Cambridge Elements ≡

Elements in Historical Theory and Practice
edited by
Daniel Woolf
Queen's University, Ontario

CONFRONTING EVIL
IN HISTORY

Daniel Little
University of Michigan

CAMBRIDGE
UNIVERSITY PRESS

Shaftesbury Road, Cambridge CB2 8EA, United Kingdom

One Liberty Plaza, 20th Floor, New York, NY 10006, USA

477 Williamstown Road, Port Melbourne, VIC 3207, Australia

314–321, 3rd Floor, Plot 3, Splendor Forum, Jasola District Centre,
New Delhi – 110025, India

103 Penang Road, #05–06/07, Visioncrest Commercial, Singapore 238467

Cambridge University Press is part of Cambridge University Press & Assessment,
a department of the University of Cambridge.

We share the University's mission to contribute to society through the pursuit of
education, learning and research at the highest international levels of excellence.

www.cambridge.org
Information on this title: www.cambridge.org/9781009108423

DOI: 10.1017/9781009104265

First published 2022

A catalogue record for this publication is available from the British Library.

ISBN 978-1-009-10842-3 Paperback
ISSN 2634-8616 (online)
ISSN 2634-8608 (print)

Confronting Evil in History

Elements in Historical Theory and Practice

DOI: 10.1017/9781009104265
First published online: September 2022

Daniel Little
University of Michigan

Author for correspondence: Daniel Little, delittle@umich.edu

Abstract: Evil is sometimes thought to be incomprehensible and abnormal, falling outside of familiar historical and human processes. And yet the twentieth century was replete with instances of cruelty on a massive scale, including systematic torture, murder, and enslavement of ordinary, innocent human beings. These overwhelming atrocities included genocide, totalitarianism, the Holocaust, and the Holodomor. This Element underlines the importance of careful, truthful historical investigation of the complicated realities of dark periods in human history; the importance of understanding these events in terms that give attention to the human experience of the people who were subject to them and those who perpetrated them; the question of whether the idea of "evil" helps us to confront these periods honestly; and the possibility of improving our civilization's resilience in the face of the impulses toward cruelty to other human beings that have so often emerged.

This Element also has a video abstract: www.cambridge.org/confrontingevil

Keywords: genocide, totalitarianism, Holocaust, historicity, atrocity

ISBNs: 9781009108423 (PB), 9781009104265 (OC)
ISSNs: 2634-8616 (online), 2634-8608 (print)

Contents

1 Introduction

The twentieth century witnessed the most sustained and devastating regimes of killing, enslavement, and degradation that the world has yet witnessed. The genocide of the Holocaust, the massive killing and degradation associated with Stalin's war of starvation against the Ukrainian countryside, and other instances of barbarous and state-initiated periods of atrocity during the century were enormous historical evils that must be confronted honestly and fully if humanity is to hope to avoid such catastrophes in the future.

Evil is sometimes thought to be incomprehensible and abnormal, falling outside of familiar historical and human processes. And yet human history is replete with instances of cruelty on a massive scale, including systematic torture, murder, and enslavement of ordinary, innocent human beings. This Element underlines the importance of careful, truthful historical investigation of the complicated realities of dark periods in our human history; the importance of understanding these events in terms that give attention to the human experience of the people who lived through them and those who perpetrated them; and the possibility of improving our civilization's resilience in the face of the impulses toward cruelty to other human beings that have so often emerged.

Vast numbers of words have been written about the atrocities of the twentieth century – about genocide, the Holocaust, Stalin's war of starvation against Ukraine's peasants, the Gulag, and about other periods of unimaginable and deliberate mass suffering throughout the century. First-person accounts, historians' narratives, sociologists' and psychologists' studies of perpetrators' behavior, novelists, filmmakers, playwrights, exhibition curators . . . all these kinds of works are available to us as vehicles for understanding what happened, and – perhaps – why. So perhaps the job of delineating and understanding the Holocaust has been done: we know what we need to know about the terrible twentieth century.

I do not agree with that view. First, there are vast areas of silence about these periods of atrocity in different regimes and countries that have resulted from both an impulse of comfortable ignorance by citizens and deliberate efforts by states and parties to conceal the truth. Further, there are large gaps between the common beliefs most literate people have about the Holocaust or Stalinist dictatorship and the massive human suffering and indignity that these events entailed. Most of us do not "understand" the Holocaust, the Holodomor, or the Gulag. I believe another perspective will be helpful – even necessary – as well, if we are to encompass this century of horror into our understanding of our human past and be prepared for a better future. This is the perspective of the philosopher – in particular, the philosopher of history.

But why so? Why is it urgent for philosophy to confront the Holocaust? What insights can philosophers bring to the rest of us about the particular evils that the twentieth century involved?

Most fundamentally, I am interested in finding appropriate ways of approaching the philosophy of history so as to arrive at a better ability to understand and confront the evils of the twentieth century. This involves raising concrete questions about how we as human beings define ourselves in the world, in light of the histories our predecessors and contemporaries have created. How should human beings of the twenty-first century relate to the evil events of the twentieth century? And how can humanity grow from confronting this history honestly? Reflecting deeply upon the history of the Holocaust or the Holodomor seriously and honestly has the potential of changing our natures, making these crimes less likely in the future. Truthful historical inquiry is crucial to our human ability to learn from the periods of atrocity and evil in the past, and to do better in the future. This recognition is fundamental to the historicity of a people's identity and is the sole source of hope for a better future for humanity.

In short, this Elements volume seeks to explore the difference that the evils of the twentieth century make for philosophy and history. The sections that follow explore three large themes: the historicity of human culture and morality; the deep and imponderable evils that human beings and their social institutions committed throughout the twentieth century; and the crucial role played in twentieth-century evil by the institutions of states. The overriding premise is the idea that "we human beings" are historical beings. Human moral culture is historically located; we create our defining values and commitments through our experiences of ordinary life and great historical events. We can become better, more compassionate, and more just, when we honestly recognize the ways in which we and our predecessors have acted horribly – often in circumstances that we can imagine applying to ourselves. An overriding commitment to truthful historical discovery and a commitment to rejecting the myths and ideologies of the past are the most important tasks for the historian of the evils of the twentieth century.

The organization of the Element brings together relevant philosophical ideas about humanity with new aspects of historians' knowledge of the evils of the twentieth century. Section 2 exposes the reader to some of the relevant ideas about human nature, culture, and society drawn from European philosophy, as well as a brief treatment of the concept of evil in use in this Element. Section 3 introduces the idea of historicized humanity, reflecting the view that human culture and institutions are fundamentally the creations of human communities and traditions. Sections 4 and 5 turn to aspects of the history of evil in the twentieth century, with central emphasis on new efforts to understand the

Holocaust in Section 4 and a focus on "lies and myths" in historical narratives about the period in Section 5. Section 6 returns to the topic of the relationship between the evils of the twentieth century and the need for a transformation in philosophy in light of the mass murder, repression, and degradation created by human beings against other human beings during just a few decades of the twentieth century.

We can affirm "Never again" only if we honestly confront the past, and work to create the moral commitments and social institutions that will make those crimes impossible in the future. Honest historical research and reckoning are crucial for this task of self-making.

2 Philosophy and Twentieth-Century Evil

The large-scale evils of the twentieth century break all our conventional under-standings of humanity, ethics, and good and evil.[1] They differ from the crimes of previous centuries by their massive scope, their embeddedness in the institu-tions of powerful states, and the intentionality and persistence of the evils committed. And yet they are part of our history as human beings and as cultures. This section considers two fundamental questions: Why should philosophy confront the history of evil in the twentieth century? And further, how should it do so? The answers to these questions cannot be adequately summarized at the start, but it will be helpful to give some idea of the thrust of the arguments to come. We then turn to the question of how to define historical evil.

First, *why* should philosophy concern itself with the facts of genocide, totalitarianism, and the Holocaust? One of the leading goals of philosophy since Socrates has been to provide a framework of concepts and principles in terms of which to understand the human condition, and often the guiding premise has been that human beings can live rational and peaceful lives. The facts of the twentieth century cast profound doubt on that idea, and with those doubts comes skepticism about underlying philosophical ideas about human nature, politics, and justice. Further, philosophers have often hoped that their theories and arguments might contribute to a better future for humanity. If philosophy is to make good on that promise, it is crucial to honestly confront

---

[1] To refer to the evils of the twentieth century in a way that encompasses the Holocaust, the Holodomor, and the Gulag may seem to invite a return to the "historians' debate" of the 1980s (Kampe 1987; Friedländer 1992; LaCapra 1997; Maier 1997) or the "comparability debate" of 2021 (Jennifer 2021; Little 2021a). Here I prefer not to enter into disputes over whether the Holocaust was wholly unique, whether the genocide of the Holocaust should be compared to the devastation of the Holodomor, or whether we must arrive at a comparative judgment of the relative evil of the totalitarianisms of Hitler and Stalin. It is enough to recognize that each of these historical occurrences was evil on a massive scale, each was unique in its own way, and each poses profound moral and civilizational issues.

the deadly and horrific realities of the human cruelties of the twentieth century, and for philosophers to adjust their theories of human nature and social life accordingly.

Second, *how* should philosophy confront the evils of the twentieth century? The perspective that will be taken here is one that emphasizes active investigation, honest reflection, and collaborative work with historians and social scientists to attempt to answer the substantive questions created by the Holocaust and the rise of totalitarianism. The goal of those honest inquiries is to assist in recognizing the sources of evil as they manifested in the twentieth century, and to arrive at credible strategies for changing our culture and our institutions in such a way as to make recurrence of pervasive evil less likely in the future. Seen in this way, philosophy should confront evil in a transformative way: How can we change our own values, our institutions, and our conceptions of ourselves in ways that serve to defeat future evil actions and plans of political leaders? Philosophy should abandon its inclinations toward a priori thought and engage deeply with historians, sociologists, social psychologists, students of political institutions, and participants in a joint effort to extirpate the seeds of hatred and massive violence from our futures.

What is Evil?

I invoke the idea of "evil" to describe the atrocities of the twentieth century. This Element is not primarily a conceptual discussion of the meaning of the concept of evil.[2] Rather, it is a reflection on the extraordinary and horrific events undertaken by states, armies, corporations, leaders, and ordinary people during the twentieth century.

One definition we might try out for "evil" in human affairs is this: *Evil actions by states or individuals are actions that deliberately lead to wanton human suffering and death on a large scale with no regard for the human value of the innocent human beings who are harmed.* Evil is *deliberate* cruelty on a *massive* scale, including systematic torture, murder, starvation, degradation, and enslavement of ordinary, *innocent human beings*.

Note that this definition draws a close connection between human agency and evil. Evil is not just a very bad and regrettable result; it is the result of human action and choice, involving the intention to create the unwarranted suffering

---

[2] Marcus Singer (2010) provides an excellent philosophical discussion of the concept of evil. He summarizes his conception in these terms: "*Evil acts*, on the conception I am developing, are acts that are horrendously wrong, that cause immense suffering and are done with an evil intention or from an evil motive, the intention or motive to do something horrendously wrong causing immense unwarranted suffering" (Singer 2010: 205).

the action produces. "Evil" is not a force unto itself. "Disembodied evil" did not create the Holocaust or the Holodomor. Instead, human actors and states created evil in their designs of extermination, enslavement, and subjection. They did these things through their own actions and through the institutions and social practices that they created, supported, and inhabited. Confronting evil does not mean confronting something outside of human agency or experience. Rather, it means confronting the horrendous actions and plans that were undertaken by human beings against other human beings.

This definition conforms reasonably well with the conceptions offered by several recent treatments by philosophers of historical evils from a secular perspective. John Kekes (2007) provides a similar definition of evil in these terms: "The evil of an action, therefore, consists in the combination of three components: the malevolent motivation of evildoers; the serious, excessive harm caused by their actions; and the lack of morally acceptable excuse for the actions" (Kekes 2007: 2). Claudia Card (2010) provides a secular account of evil that emphasizes inexcusability: "Briefly, the modifications are (1) that evils are inexcusable, not just culpable, (2) that evils need not be extraordinary (probably most are not), and (3) that not all institutional evil implies individual culpability" (Card 2010: 4). Susan Neiman (2002) offers an ostensive account of the concept of evil, writing that "Auschwitz, by contrast, stands for all that is meant when we use the word evil today: absolute wrongdoing that leaves no room for account or expiation" (Neiman 2002: 3). Each of these definitions identifies an important feature of the acts and events of the twentieth century that are of central concern here.

Particularly noteworthy for my arguments here is the emphasis that Kekes places on "decency" and "moral imagination." These features of moral psychology are at the center of what is needed if we are to learn from the historical experience of evil.

> It is reasonable to conclude, then, that if moral imagination had enabled evildoers to understand better their victims and their own motives and to realize that they had attractive alternatives to evildoing, then they would have been less likely to become or to continue as evildoers .... Moderately intelligent people have the capacity of moral imagination, but like other modes of imagination, it has to be cultivated. (Kekes 2007: 237)

For Kekes, then, committing evil derives at least in part from an insufficiency of moral imagination and a failure to recognize the reality of other persons. We can cultivate moral imagination by paying attention to the realities of the experience of other human beings – through our personal experience, through literature, and through the horrors of the histories of the Cathar Crusade or the

My Lai massacre.[3] Human beings are not fixed in their moral capabilities; rather, we can gain compassion and resist the impulses toward participating in evil actions.

This observation about the cultivation of moral imagination points in the direction of a view of how it is possible to learn from history. Confronting the horrific circumstances of the massacres of the Cathars, the deliberate starvation of Ukrainian peasants in 1932, or the murder of innocent Vietnamese villagers in My Lai in 1968, unavoidably brings us to a more vivid understanding of the moral evil of those events: the pain, suffering, and loss that these actions created for human beings much like ourselves. The strongest impression one might take away from Hannah Arendt's (2006) account of the trial of Eichmann is the utter lack of sympathy, pity, or compassion Eichmann showed for the victims of his activities (Stangneth 2014). Atrocities often depend on the total dehumanization of the victims, and compassion makes it more difficult to accomplish that trick.

Susan Neiman introduces a key element of historicity into her discussion of evil. Her treatment of Rousseau emphasizes Rousseau's view of the malleability of human nature and emotions such as compassion (Neiman 2002: 44). Neiman finds that our historical actions – our human and collective actions over time – have both created evil events and have created the grounds for reducing or eliminating evil. These ideas are suggestive for the question of how to confront the historical realities of evil, because they point to the fundamental malleability of human culture and morality. Human nature and history are reciprocally intertwined. And this malleability in turn suggests the possibility of the kind of "self-positing" and learning from history that is most relevant to the approach to evil taken here when it comes to bringing historical understanding into productive conversation with the extreme evils and atrocities of the twentieth century.

Consider finally the remarks on evil offered by the philosopher and critic Terry Eagleton. Eagleton (2010) develops his treatment of the concept of evil largely through examples of evil actions from literature. He believes that we can learn a good deal about this feature of the human condition from fiction writers who grapple with horrific actions by individuals – murder, rape, acts of senseless and unprovoked violence. A limitation of Eagleton's analysis is that it focuses almost entirely on the horrific actions of specific isolated individuals, and it emphasizes the "irrational" nature of these actions. It is not evident that this orientation gives a basis for understanding the actions of a Stalin, an Eichmann, or a compliant member of an Order Police unit

---

[3] Brief descriptions of the Cathar Crusade and several other instances of atrocity are provided in the next section.

assigned to hunting and killing Ukrainian Jews. More illuminating are the narratives of observers of the concrete horrors of the Holocaust or the Holodomor; for example, Vasily Grossman's account of Treblinka (2010). What, then, is the value of reading literature when we attempt to think about evil? It is tempting to believe that we learn more from literature about the victims of evil actions rather than their perpetrators. As Martha Nussbaum (1996) emphasizes, a novelist is often able to bring the reader into a more acute relationship of empathy and compassion for the victims of evil actions than the journalist or the historian. And this experience, for the reader, may permit him or her to broaden the moral imagination through which he sees and interprets massacre, enslavement, and torture.

The idea that evil actions are "irrational" is also suspect. Eagleton sometimes seems to support this notion: "Let us return, then, to the question of whether evil is best seen as a kind of purposeless or nonpragmatic wickedness. In one sense, the answer is surely yes. Evil is not primarily concerned with practical consequences. As the French psychoanalyst André Green writes, 'Evil is without 'why' because its *raison d'être* is to proclaim that everything which exists has no meaning, obeys no order, pursues no aim, depends only on the power it can exercise to impose its will on the objects of its appetite'" (Eagleton 2010: 103). However, the actions that are of central concern in this Element – genocide, Holocaust, totalitarian terror, the Gulag – were far from unmotivated or nondeliberate. On the contrary, Himmler, Beria, and the Gulag guard all had reasons for their actions; and their reasons were part of the constituents of the evil of their actions.

Historical Examples of Evil

This Element is primarily concerned with the horrendous events of the twentieth century. It is clear, however, that evil and atrocity occurred throughout human history, and in places other than Europe. Several specific examples are mentioned in the sections that follow, and it will be useful to provide brief descriptions of them here.

Consider first the Melian massacre, described by Thucydides in his history of the Peloponnesian War (1998). In 416 BCE during the Peloponnesian War between Athens and Sparta, an Athenian naval force attacked the island city-state of Melos. Melos was neutral in the war between Athens and Sparta but was perceived by the Athenians to be friendly to Sparta. The Athenian force demanded the unconditional surrender of the city-state or face complete destruction. Melos refused to surrender immediately, but eventually surrendered following a crippling siege by the Athenian forces. Following the surrender all the men were killed and the women and children were sold into slavery. The actions by the Athenians following continuing resistance by the Melians are described by Thucydides:

> Reinforcements afterwards arriving from Athens in consequence, under the command of Philocrates, son of Demeas, the siege was now pressed vigorously; and some treachery taking place inside, the Melians surrendered at discretion to the Athenians, who put to death all the grown men whom they took, and sold the women and children for slaves, and subsequently sent out five hundred colonists and inhabited the place themselves. (Thucydides 1998: book V, chapter XVII; Little 2021b)

The Cathar Crusade took place in southern France for almost two decades at the start of the thirteenth century. Instigated by Pope Innocent III to extinguish the heresy of "Catharism," it led to the conquest of many towns in Languedoc, and the subsequent infliction of horrendous torture, mutilation, starvation, and murder of the innocent people who fell victim to the crusading armies. In Brezier, the first town conquered, 20,000 people were executed. John Kekes (2007) writes, "The Army of God massacred about twenty thousand men, women, and children, faithful Catholics and heretical Cathars, and then, for good measure, burned down the town" (Kekes 2007: 13). Kekes documents the maiming and mutilation that were commonplace during this period of intense violence. The murder and mutilation of thousands of innocent people by rampaging crusader armies continued for almost twenty years.

A third horrendous example of massive historical evil was the Holodomor, Stalin's deliberate war of starvation against Ukrainian rural society in the early 1930s. The facts are grim and horrific and were first described in detail by historian Robert Conquest (1986). Stalin's state enforced a process of rural collectivization aimed at destroying the "kulak" class by confiscating essentially all the grain in the region, leading to mass starvation. Lynne Viola (2005) makes it clear that these actions were part of a "revolution from above" – an effort to impose collective ownership on agriculture throughout the territory of the Union of Soviet Socialist Republics (USSR), to create communism rapidly. These actions and strategies were a war against the peasantry – a deliberate effort to destroy and exterminate a whole social group. Violence by the OGPU (secret police) intensified under the direction of Genrikh Yagoda. Arrests and mass deportations to labor camps in the north ensued, leading to mass deaths. Applebaum (2017) estimates that at least 3.9 million Ukrainians died of starvation by the end of 1934 (Little 2021c).

A fourth example of massive evil is the "rape of Nanjing" in 1937. This atrocity took place against the noncombatant population of the Chinese city of

Nanjing by a Japanese army during Japan's war of conquest against China. After the Japanese army conquered the city of Nanjing in December, 1937, a horrific period of killings, torture, mutilation, and rape resulted in the deaths of between 260,000 and 350,000 innocent and unarmed civilians. Iris Chang describes the weeks of terror and murder in Nanjing in these terms: "When the city fell on December 13, 1937, Japanese soldiers began an orgy of cruelty seldom if ever matched in world history" (Chang 1997: 4). There was no military purpose to the killings and torture; rather, commanders, officers, and ordinary soldiers seem to have given themselves over to an unconstrained and entirely nonrational thirst for imposing suffering and death. War crimes trials were instituted after the end of World War II under jurisdiction of the International Military Tribunal for the Far East, leading to conviction of several high military officials for their direct or indirect responsibility for this slaughter.

A final example is the My Lai massacre during the United States' conduct of the Vietnam War. In March 1968 a company of US infantry soldiers entered the Vietnamese village of My Lai. Their combat mission was to locate and engage with a group of Viet Cong soldiers in a "search and destroy" mission. There were no Viet Cong troops in the village. This mission resulted in a major and unprovoked massacre of hundreds of innocent civilians and represents one of the most terrible instances of war atrocities in recent US history (Howard Jones 2017). Under the command of Lieutenant William Calley the company searched the village. No Viet Cong soldiers or significant caches of weapons were found, but the noncombatant residents of the village were gathered together, and under orders from Lieutenant Calley, soldiers in the company killed over 500 villagers. Lieutenant Calley himself killed many villagers with a machine gun. An unknown number of women were raped by members of the company. The killing stopped only when a US army helicopter pilot, Warrant Officer Hugh Thompson, witnessing the killing below him, landed his aircraft between soldiers and villagers, and demanded at gunpoint a stop to the killing. Though there is uncertainty about the exact number of victims, Howard Jones accepts the estimate of 504 victims, including 182 women, and 173 children and infants. (The official US army investigation concluded in 1970 that there were between 175 and 400 victims, but later estimates appear to be more reliable; Peers 1970.) The massacre was concealed by senior military officers but became public through the efforts of a fellow infantryman not involved in the massacre who attempted to make the massacre known. Eventually the massacre came to wide public knowledge through journalism by Seymour Hersh (1970). Fourteen men were charged with crimes, including Lieutenant Calley, and only Calley was convicted. His prison sentence was commuted by President Richard Nixon after serving only three years.

Each of these historical events is all but incomprehensible to a humane observer. The cruelty, injustice, and lack of compassion that each episode reflects is impossible to reconcile with any conception of the fundamental compassion of human beings for their fellow human beings. Each is an instance of historical evil. Each has its own social and ideological setting, and each requires careful historical investigation. However, with the exception of the Ukrainian famine, none reaches the scope and intentionality of the crimes of states in the twentieth century that we will examine in greater detail in the second part of this Element. The crimes of genocide, enslavement, and totalitarian dictatorship of the twentieth century appear to fall in a different category of evil altogether.

The Evil of Genocide

Many terrible things happened in the twentieth century. Most horrible, and most difficult to assimilate into any existing conception of warfare or atrocity, was the crime of genocide: the Nazi regime's Final Solution of the "Jewish Question," articulated in the Wannsee Conference as an action plan for murdering all of Europe's Jews. The Shoah was not the first genocide in the twentieth century. The sustained campaign of mass slaughter of the Armenians in the final stages of the Ottoman Empire took place in 1915–1916, resulting in between 664,000 and 1.2 million deaths (Kévorkian 2011). But the Nazi genocide against Europe's Jews captures all aspects of the definition of evil sketched in section 1 above: "Evil actions by states or individuals are actions that deliberately lead to wanton human suffering and death on a large scale with no regard for the human value of the innocent human beings who are harmed." The mass killings by gunfire of the Jews of Ukraine, Poland, Lithuania, and other eastern European territories that took place at the hands of the *Einsatzgruppen* units and their non-German collaborators in 1941 and 1942 marked the beginning of a campaign of industrialized murder against a whole people – women, men, and children. This campaign continued through the deportation of Europe's Jews to extermination camps in many areas of German control, including Auschwitz and Treblinka in Poland. Further, as Vasily Grossman insisted in 1943 in "Ukraine without Jews" (2011), this campaign amounted to more than a monstrous sum of murders of innocent individuals; it amounted to the murder and extinction of a people and its traditions, cultures, music, and values.

A large literature has arisen encompassing the perspectives of historians, social scientists, and literary specialists on the topic of genocide: how to define it, how to explain it, and how to commemorate its victims. The diverse range of approaches to research in the field of genocide studies is well represented in the *Oxford Handbook of Genocide Studies* (Bloxham and Moses 2010). The volume *Understanding Atrocities* (Murray and Powell 2017) contains a wealth of important material, and the editors emphasize the evolution of genocide studies in terms of its growing transdisciplinarity: "A key feature of the scholarly study of genocide has been a steady broadening of perspectives, beginning with efforts to look beyond the universality of the Holocaust as the genocide" (preface). Of particular interest to the question of how to study the Holocaust is the collection *New directions in genocide research* (Adam Jones 2012), which contains a range of valuable materials from the conceptual to the sociologically detailed case study. The volume also introduces issues of gender and environment into the discussion. Hundreds of specialized monographs have been published in the field of genocide studies, ranging from detailed studies of specific massacres (Burds 2013) to the role of business in the Final Solution (Allen 2002). Valuable research results are published in a wide range of specialized journals, including *Holocaust and Genocide Studies* (Oxford), *International Journal of Transitional Justice*, and *Genocide Studies and Prevention*. Taken as a whole, this literature represents a dynamic and sustained transdisciplinary effort to achieve concrete and detailed understanding of the atrocities of genocide, with concrete hypotheses about how national and international institutions can be better secured against such crimes in the future.

A Role for Philosophy

Let us now return to the question, why does philosophy need to confront the profound evils of the twentieth century? There are at least two important reasons. First, Western philosophy has commonly involved theories of society and politics that emphasize rationality and the good. Philosophers want to know what conditions constitute a happy human life, a just state, and a harmonious society. And philosophers usually work on assumptions that lead, eventually, back to the idea of human rationality and a degree of benevolence. Human beings are assumed to be deliberative about their own lives and courses of action; they have concern for the lives and suffering of others; they want to live in a harmonious society; they are capable of recognizing "fair" social arrangements and institutions; and they have some degree of motivation to support such institutions.[4] These assumptions attach especially strongly to philosophers such as Aristotle, Seneca, Locke, Rousseau, Kant, and Hegel; less strongly to Hobbes, Machiavelli, and Nietzsche; and perhaps not at all to Heidegger. But there is a strong and recurrent theme of rationality and benevolence that underlies much of the tradition of Western philosophy. The facts about the Holocaust, the Holodomor, or the Armenian or Rwandan genocides do not conform to this assumption of rational human goodness. Or rather, rationality and benevolence fall apart; instrumental rationality is divorced from a common attachment to the human good, and rational means are chosen to bring about suffering, enslavement, and death to millions of individual human beings. The Holocaust, then, forces philosophers to ask themselves: what is a human being, if groups of human beings are capable of such deliberate cruelty, degradation, and murder of their fellows?

The two ideas highlighted here – rationality and benevolence – need some further explication. Philosophers are not economists; they do not think of rationality as purely a matter of instrumental cleverness in fitting means to achieving one's ends. Pure economic rationality is "atomistic," in the sense that it considers only the particular individual's preferences and beliefs. Rather, part of the tradition of Western political philosophy has a more substantive under-standing of rationality: to be rational includes the ability to recognize the reality of other human beings; to recognize the reality of their aspirations and vulner-abilities; and to have a degree of motivation to contribute to their thriving. Thomas Nagel describes this view of rationality in *The Possibility of Altruism* (1970). Likewise, Amartya Sen embraces a conception of reason that includes sociality and a recognition of the reality of other human beings (Sen 1977; Sen 1999). This is a "relational" theory of rationality, encompassing the idea that human beings exist in a social context and in relation and coordination with other human beings.

Benevolence too requires comment. Benevolence – or what Nagel refers to as altruism – is a rational motivation that derives from a recognition of the reality and importance of other persons' lives – their life plans, their happiness and

---

[4] One reason for this inclination derives from a traditional philosophical urge toward universality and abstraction. Since Socrates, Plato, and Aristotle students of philosophy have been offered the most general possible questions: "What is virtue?," "What is happiness?," "What is wisdom?," or "What is justice?". This leads philosophers from Aristotle to Locke, Kant, and Rawls to engage in "ideal" political theorizing, without paying attention to the empirical and historical variations that exist. Rawls (1971) is fully explicit that his theory of justice falls in the range of ideal theory rather than empirically complex actual political settings. But it should be apparent that general and universal theories are of little use in understanding and confronting genocide, slavery, or tyranny. Rather, we need to have historically and empirically informed understandings of particular instances, if we are to arrive at theories and remedies. What are the social and institutional circumstances in which atrocity, genocide, and tyranny are likely to emerge?

suffering, their fulfillment. To be benevolent is to have a degree of motivation to care about the lives of others, and to contribute to social arrangements that serve everyone to some degree. As Kant (1959) puts the point in one version of the categorical imperative in *Foundations of the Metaphysics of Morals*, "treat others as ends, not merely as means." The point of this principle is fundamental: rationality requires recognition of the fundamental reality of the lives, experiences, and fulfillment of others. Benevolence does not mean that one must become Alyosha in Dostoyevsky's *Brothers Karamazov*, selflessly devoted to the needs of others. But it does mean that the happiness and misery, life and death, of the other is important to oneself. Thomas Nagel puts the point very strongly: strict egoism is as irrational as solipsism.[5]

If the underlying philosophical anthropology that has guided much Western philosophy involves the assumptions of relational rationality, benevolence, and a concern for justice, then the experience of the twentieth century must be recognized as an enormous challenge to that philosophical anthropology. In place of benevolence, much of the world experienced hatred at the individual and collective levels; in place of altruistic rationality, large populations were prepared to accept the dehumanization and murder of their neighbors and distant strangers; and in place of secure commitment to principles of equality and rights, brutal fascist and totalitarian regimes found wide popular support.

This brings us to the crucial point: the murderous anti-Semitism of the Nazi period, the deliberate and intentional plan to exterminate the Jews from all of Europe, and Stalin's war on his own people – all of this is fundamentally incompatible with the idea that human beings are generally and by their nature "rationally benevolent." Ordinary German policemen were indeed willing to kill Jews at the instruction of their superiors, and then enjoy the evening singing beer songs with their friends. Ordinary Poles were willing to assault and kill their neighbors. Ordinary French citizens were willing to betray their Jewish neighbors to Vichy police. How can philosophy come to grips with these basic facts about individual human behavior from the twentieth century?

In short, the facts of atrocity, genocide, enslavement, and tyranny force philosophers to provide more historically situated theories of human morality, communality, and rationality. Certainly it remains possible to maintain that

---

[5] The phenomenological grounding of human ethics provided by Emmanuel Levinas requires mention here as well. Deriving from Husserl's phenomenology, Levinas offers a conception of "self" and "other" that fully rejects the atomistic, individualistic inclinations of the social contract tradition of social ethics. Levinas holds that recognition of the other creates boundless, enduring obligations between self and other (Levinas 1969, 2003). This stance gives ontological priority to human beings in relationships with each other, rather than to disinterested autonomous agents. Levinas was himself a Lithuanian survivor of the Holocaust, and after 1945 he engaged his philosophical ideas with the task of remembering and understanding the Holocaust.

human beings are *capable* of rational benevolence; but it is unavoidable that philosophy must recognize the dark sides of human capacities embodied in the tragedies of the twentieth century: suspicion and hatred of other groups, self-serving motivations, failures of courage. Social philosophy needs to be reintroduced to social psychology. The "ordinary men" whom Christopher Browning (1992) describes in the Order Police (Section 4) are far from the rationally benevolent, justice-seeking individuals who populate the tradition of liberal political philosophy. This suggests that political and social theorizing by philosophers urgently needs greater engagement with the findings of historians and social scientists about the real social processes that facilitated genocide, totalitarianism, and enslavement.

The second reason that philosophy needs to confront honestly the facts of the twentieth century is more constructive. Perhaps philosophy has some of the resources needed to construct a better vision of the world for the future, that will make the ideal of a society of rationally benevolent citizens more feasible and stable. Perhaps, by once recognizing the terrible traps that ensnared Germans, Poles, Ukrainians, Lithuanians, and Russians, social and political philosophy can modestly contribute to a vision of a more stable future in which genocide, enslavement, and extermination are no longer possible, or at least unlikely. Perhaps there is a constructive role for political and social philosophy in the twenty-first century. And, if this is to be possible, it must be expressible in convincing terms to a broad democratic populace, so that ordinary citizens can have genuine and resilient convictions about their liberties, the equality of all human beings, and a willingness to act collectively in defense of these values and their fellow citizens.

There is another side of this coin: perhaps the history of philosophy is itself interspersed with a framework of ideas that has perpetuated racism, anti-Semitism, and bigotry – and thereby perhaps contributed to the evils of the twentieth century. Michael Mack (2003) argues in *German Idealism and the Jew: The Inner Anti-Semitism of Philosophy and German Jewish Responses* that negative assumptions about Jews come into Immanuel Kant's writings in a very deep way. He argues that Kant represents Jews as "heteronomous," whereas ethical life requires "autonomy." These statements are anti-Semitic on their face, and Mack argues that they are not simply superficial prejudices of the age, but rather are premises that Kant was willing to defend. Bernard Boxill makes similar claims about Kant's moral philosophy with regard to racism. Boxill believes that Kant's philosophical anthropology leads him to a position that is committed to racial hierarchies among human beings (Boxill 2017). These concerns show that philosophy needs to be self-critical; philosophers need to ask whether some of the sources of twentieth-century evil may have been embedded in the tradition of philosophy itself. Slavery, racism, anti-Semitism, gender oppression, and colonial rule by Europeans seem to have cognates within the traditions of Western philosophy.[6]

There is a final reason why philosophy needs to engage seriously with evil in the twentieth century: philosophy is meant to *matter* in human life. The hope for philosophy, offered by Socrates and Seneca, Hume and Rousseau, is that the explorations of philosophers can contribute to better lives and greater human fulfillment for humanity. This suggests that philosophy has a duty to engage with the most difficult challenges in human life, throughout history, and to do so in ways that help to clarify and enhance human values. The evils of the twentieth century create an enormous problem of understanding for every thoughtful person. What is of concern here is not primarily a theological question – "How could a benevolent deity permit such atrocities?" – but rather a philosophical challenge – "How can we as full human beings, with our moral and imaginative capacities, confront these evils honestly, and have hope for the future?"[7] And it is a political question – how can we develop and sustain a citizenry that is strongly committed to securing the conditions of an egalitarian democracy, with political institutions that support that consensus? If philosophy cannot contribute to answering this question, then perhaps it is not fundamentally important.

The Philosophy of History

Here I will position these questions within the philosophy of history. (See Little 2020 for a more extensive account of the domain of the philosophy of history.) The Holocaust and the Holodomor are extended episodes in history, and historians seek to understand the past. Moreover, our understanding of history is also our understanding of our own humanity. But if these questions belong there, then we need a rather different view of the philosophy of history than either analytic or Continental philosophers have generally offered. Analytic philosophers have generally approached the topic of the philosophy of history from an epistemological point of view: what can we know about the past, and how? Continental philosophers (as well as speculative and theological philosophers) have offered large theories of history ("Does history have meaning?"

---

[6] Laurie Shrage urges philosophers to carefully consider the social content and context of their theories, writing, "By understanding the history of our field as a social and cultural phenomenon, and not as a set of ideas that transcend their human contexts, we will be in a better position to set a future course for our discipline" (Shrage 2008: 125).

[7] As this contrast suggests, the perspective taken here is naturalistic and historical: human beings exist within a world of culture and technology that they have collective created over time. From this point of view, religious beliefs are simply part of culture, not an external cause of human affairs (for good or evil).

"Does history have direction?") that have little to do with the concrete under-standings that we need to gain from specific historical investigations (Paul 2015). Since the 1970s the philosophy of history has stepped over the boundar-ies of both analytic and Continental traditions by raising a new set of questions about narrative and objectivity in history. Since Hayden White's (1973) mani-festo proclaiming the irreducible multiplicity of historical narratives of episodes and periods, philosophers and historians have been led to debate the meaning of "objectivity" in historical writing and to doubt the idea of historical truth. This line of thought found further expression in the work of Frank Ankersmit (1995) and his formulation of a "new philosophy of history." However, the linguistic turn in the philosophy of history is not fully satisfactory. The facts, processes, and outcomes of the Final Solution are not a postmodern drama suitable for wildly conflicting interpretations. Rather, we must demand of historians their strongest and most intellectually responsible efforts to sort out what happened, and why. We need to learn as much as we can about the historical truth about these evils, and study of the historical research currently underway supports confidence that this is attainable.[8] More satisfactory is the "postnarrativist" framework offered by Jouni-Matti Kuukkanen (2015), who provides an excel-lent philosophical account of a way of thinking about historical knowledge that is neither narrowly empiricist nor subjectivist. Kuukkanen is committed, as am I, to "the notion of rationality and rational evaluation" when it comes to historical narratives (Kuukkanen 2015: 3).

None of the existing frameworks of the philosophy of history are perfectly positioned to consider the implications of the Holocaust or other evils of the twentieth century. A philosophy of history that considers the evil of the Holocaust and the pervasive footprint of evil in the twentieth century will need to ask new questions about history and humanity, and it will need to engage in reflective deliberation about circumstances of the concrete human condition that made these horrible historical outcomes possible. Further, it will need to be one that incorporates the best thinking and writings of gifted historians and sociologists. It must join philosophy *and* history.

---

[8] Saul Friedländer's (1992) introduction to *Probing the Limits of Representation* provides a fine context for Hayden White's philosophical position on historical indeterminacy into the context of Holocaust studies. Many of the essays in the volume support the attainability of (partially) true accounts of episodes of evil during this period. A 2005 debate between Dirk Moses (Moses 2005) and Hayden White (White 2005) demonstrates that disagreements persist between historians who maintain the goal of providing approximately true accounts of important historical events and postmodernists who regard every telling of the event as an ideologically framed narrative. Moses expresses his defense of the former position, arguing instead for what he calls "bridging narra-tives" (Moses 2005: 329).

What might that new philosophy of history look like? It would be morally serious, recognizing the important connection that exists between knowledge of history and the making of humanity. It would absorb the insights of evidence-based inquiry that lie at the heart of analytic philosophy of history. It would be evidence based and would affirm the possibility of the objectivity of historical knowledge and expressing (partial) truths about important historical events. (The qualifier is important; as we will see, there are always new questions that can be posed for an important historical event, so no account represents the full and complete narrative or description of the event.) It would be collaborative with the social and behavioral sciences, understanding that historical processes unfold according to mechanisms and dynamics that have been studied in depth by sociologists, social psychologists, political scientists, and others. It would be interpretive and hermeneutic, in the sense that it represents historical events as the result of meaningful human actions. And it would be socially engaged, in the sense that it makes sustained efforts to help humanity, leaders, young people, and future generations to better understand the crimes and errors of past eras, and to think and act differently in the present. This brief description encompasses some of each of the currents of contemporary philosophy of history, but it rearranges the priorities and organization of the discipline as a whole in a way that makes for a greater readiness for confronting evil.

3 Historicizing Human Culture

Human beings are historical beings. We have constructed our identities, our value systems, and our aspirations through our actions and memories over time and the stories we tell about our past. Further, we have constructed important social and political institutions through which we pursue various human ends. Some of those institutions lead to catastrophe (the Nazi state and the *Wehrmacht*, the Soviet dictatorship and the NKVD (the Soviet secret police)), and others demonstrate resilience and provide a buffer against the evil intentions of some human beings against others. Truthful historical inquiry is crucial to our human ability to learn from the periods of atrocity and evil in the past, and to do better in the future. This recognition is fundamental to the historicity of a people's identity and social and political environment, and this capacity for creative self-transformation is perhaps the sole source of hope for a better future for humanity. In particular, this view rejects the idea that "human nature" is fixed and unchanging; that there is a single uniquely correct system of moral principles; and that human evolutionary history dictates human values and morality.

This section undertakes to explain the underpinnings of this view of human values and institutions.

Historicism and Culture Change

A key premise of this Element is the historicity of humanity: human beings have created their cultures, values, and schemes of interpretation through historical experience. Moral philosophers have often written of morality as if there were a suprahuman scheme of moral laws to which human actions should conform. Such a scheme was thought to be timeless and unchanging. Kant, for example, argued that moral obligations follow from the structure of rationality itself, the dictates of "pure practical reason." The utilitarians (Bentham, Mill, Sidgwick) held that moral obligations are defined by the principle of maximizing happiness – whether in the time of Socrates or Dietrich Bonhoeffer. In each case, the philosopher maintained that moral principles were timeless and could be discovered through abstract philosophical reflection.

However, it is entirely unbelievable to imagine that philosophy and pure reason can discover an a priori, timeless system of moral truths. Values and norms are created by human beings living in concrete social circumstances. Rather, moral philosophy should be understood as a dialogue with the moral culture of a time and place, rather than as an attempt to discover moral certainties valid beyond human experience. Dialogue, debate, and reflection are the avenues through which convergence around more basic moral ideas can emerge among persons or groups who initially disagree sharply with each other. Webb Keane's (2016) treatment of "affordances" (shared metaphors) as a way of arriving at a degree of moral agreement points in the same direction. (Keane's views are discussed later in this section.) Seen in this way, the "reflective equilibrium" approach to moral epistemology advocated by John Rawls (1971) is a plausible way of understanding the epistemic status of moral principles. This is a coherentist rather than a foundationalist epistemology, involving an ongoing adjustment of specific judgments and more general principles until a reasonable level of consistency is achieved. Moreover, if human beings' considered judgments or moral sensibilities change over time – if tormenting animals for entertainment is accepted in 1600 but largely rejected in 1900 – then the moral theory that corresponds to this system of judgments and principles will be different as well.

The premise of this Element, by contrast with philosophical universalism, is that culture and morality are human creations, and show great variation over time and space. This feature of human existence gives rise to the crucial role played by historians in the creation of culture and morality. Thucydides helped to create the "Athenian" moral framework, through his painstaking historical narrative of the Peloponnesian War. Or more exactly: Thucydides both expressed the Athenian worldview and tested and extended it through his account of the experience of Athens in its prolonged war against Sparta. David Hume's *History of England* (1975 [1754–1762]) set a moral context featuring freedom and a constitution for British subjects and rulers. Joseph Conrad's historical novel *Heart of Darkness* (2002) offered its readers a radically different vision of the meaning of European imperialism. And David Halberstam did much to change the American public's thinking about the war in Vietnam by shedding light on the lies of the US administration in *The Best and the Brightest* (1972). In each case the historian probed the concrete moral issues involved in a time and place, and helped his or her readers to seek to reconcile current beliefs and values with the facts of the historical case.[9]

There are strong philosophical antecedents for rejecting the traditional universalistic view of human nature, morality, and culture. One important thinker in this vein was Johannes Gottfried von Herder (1744–1803). Herder (1968) advocated for a historicist philosophy of human nature: the idea that human nature is itself a historical product and that human beings think and act differently in different periods of historical development. The logical implication of historicism is that human individuals become specific culturally instantiated persons through their immersion in a culture at a time. This position denies all forms of "essentialism" about human nature and about the characteristics of a people or a culture. Cultures and their value systems are contingent, and the human individuals to whom they give rise are contingently different from their predecessors and successors in other generations. But cultures themselves are in turn embodied and changed by the individuals who make them up over time. Human beings thus create themselves through history by creating cultures, norms, and schemes of thinking. National and cultural identities are themselves historically located and historically malleable.[10]

What do we mean by "culture"? Most fundamentally, we might say that a culture is defined by the frameworks of meaning, normative values, and prescribed forms of social interaction through which human beings understand their own lives and their relationships with other human beings. Clifford Geertz offers a conception of culture defined as "webs of significance he himself has spun" (Geertz 1971: 5), and Geertz spent much of his career demonstrating how

---

[9] The field of transitional justice is highly relevant to the philosophical challenges of this Element. It is a field of research dedicated to learning from atrocity and trauma in the past; absorbing the lessons of those periods; recognizing the suffering of the victims; and finding practical ways of making similar atrocities less likely in the future. This field takes very seriously the role that history and historical research can play in helping to form the moral identities of a generation of young people who have greater compassion for others (Cole 2007; Stan and Nedelsky 2013).

[10] Sonia Sikka (2011) provides an excellent discussion of this aspect of Herder's philosophy: culture, nation, "a people," and a historicist approach to the concept of human nature. Michael Forster's book *Herder's Philosophy* (2018) offers a clear and detailed exposition of Herder's philosophy.

different those interpretive frameworks are from one population to another. We might define a norm as a *socially embodied* and *individually perceived imperative* that such-and-so an action must be performed in such-and-so a fashion. Examples include "promises should be kept," "neighbors should help each other in times of need," and "people should not be cruel to animals." A scheme of values is related both to norms and meanings. It is an embodied set of practical concerns that human beings care about and around which they strive to orient their actions and life plans. For example, we might observe that one community values human well-being, the equality of all human beings, and the importance of a just system of social cooperation, while another community values hierarchy and patriarchal gender relations.

Webb Keane's (2016) boundary-breaking analysis of the role of morality and ethics in human societies brings an ethnographer's awareness of cultural speci-ficity to a broader consideration of neuroscience, developmental psychology, and evolutionary biology as well as engagement with philosophy and the human sciences. Keane's treatment is broadly compatible with the historicist interpret-ation of morality and culture offered here, and Keane gives due weight to the role of human agency in the development and application of moral ideas and "affordances" (loosely, metaphors and stereotyped examples that help people decide what to do). Keane's appeal to the natural sciences in this context reflects his understanding that human social capabilities have a natural basis in their evolutionary history and neurocognitive systems. These features set limits to the range of symbolic and normative systems that human communities can create. His consideration of morality and ethics from the perspectives of the historical sciences reflects his conviction that the range of variation of symbolic and normative systems feasible for human societies is broad, and the evidence of historical sociology and ethnography of multiple cultures bears this out.

It is important to emphasize that the components of culture are both socially embodied and internally represented within the individual. A community embodies its norms, values, and meanings collectively through its instruction of the young and its inducements and sanctions to the noncompliant. An individual embodies norms and meanings through his or her own mental, cognitive, and emotional frameworks of interpretation and action. The two perspectives on culture are linked: individuals who have "learned" the ambient culture help to convey it to others; and the community of individuals into which one is born "teaches" the neophyte in how to behave, how to think, and how to interpret the world around him or her.

Organized religions have advocated for specific "codes of conduct" for practitioners, followers, or even all human beings. Religious codes of conduct are usually based on revealed authority rather than philosophical argument – the authority of the Koran or the Bible, authority of the founders, or authority of specialists who speak for the divine beings. But assuming a naturalistic view of the world, it is reasonable to take the view that the religious codes of a time are expressions of the ambient moral attitudes of the time, perhaps with innovations introduced by charismatic teachers and leaders. Religious moral prescriptions rest upon the practical sets of social and interpersonal norms that exist in the communities in which these groups and bodies of doctrine emerged.

If we take a naturalistic view of humanity, then there is also an evolutionary question to be posed. What is it about the evolutionary history of primates that has led to the evolution of an organism that is capable of normative behavior? Is there an evolutionary dimension to the moral emotions (or the underlying cognitive capacities that permit the embodiment of moral emotions)? Is an inclination to compassion or fairness "in our genes" in some way? Allan Gibbard's (1990) philosophical analysis of these questions is especially nuanced and serves well to rebut crude forms of sociobiology (the idea that human moral and behavioral characteristics are hard wired as a result of our evolutionary history). Gibbard's view is that the evolutionary history of primates took place in a setting of social groups, where psychological capacities supporting cooperation were favored because they possessed selection advantage. The evolutionary history of primates (including *homo sapiens*) resulted in a species that had a range of psychological tools or capacities that could be activated or deployed in a wide variety of ways. This prepared *homo sapiens* to become a "cultural animal," capable of creating and living within social groups and cultural systems. And this process of creation had a great deal of flexibility – as human technological and linguistic capabilities also demonstrated great flexibility. Significantly, Gibbard's view leaves a great deal of room for "plasticity" in the moral emotions and the normative systems that are embodied in concrete social traditions and groups. (Keane supports this view as well; Keane 2016: 30).[11]

A particularly important question for this approach is the topic of culture change. Are there processes through which the moral framework of a time changes and – perhaps – improves? For example, is there a moment of transition between generations when "sympathy for one's kin" becomes more generalized and becomes "sympathy for one's neighbors," and eventually "sympathy for distant human beings"? Is it possible for a human population to "bootstrap" its way to a more benevolent and just way of living, through gradual change in the moral attitudes of individuals? What kinds of

---

[11] The eminent evolutionary biologist Richard Lewontin (1992) supports this view as well. He argues for the idea that human beings are the product of a long evolutionary process but rejects entirely the idea that this fact has strong implications for human morality.

effort and lived experience and learning might have the effect of *improving* the moral culture of a civilization in the making? Can human communities and cultures learn from their mistakes? Can the honest study of history enhance this process of cultural learning?

There appear to be at least two concrete levers that might allow for moral learning by a historically situated community. The first is an extension of *empathy and compassion* beyond its current borders. We can define compassion briefly in these terms: the ability to perceive the suffering experience of another person, and to be motivated to help that person avoid the suffering. Further, we might speculate that this is an emotion that human beings learn through experience and reflection. The moral intuitions of a community may change when individuals are brought to recognize in greater fullness the lived experience and capacities for happiness and suffering in other human beings; individuals may broaden their compassion for more distant strangers.

The philosopher who has shed the most light on compassion is Martha Nussbaum. In "Compassion: The Basic Social Emotion" (1996; see also 2001) she explores the importance that compassion and pity play in the moral ordering of human social life. Nussbaum regards compassion as a prerequisite moral emotion for much of social life; and she believes that it must be learned. Moreover, literature, drama, and history can be crucial components of that learning.[12] Nussbaum argues that compassion is a crucial part of interpersonal knowledge: "compassion, in the philosophical tradition, is a central bridge between the individual and the community; it is conceived of as our species' way of hooking the interests of others to our own personal goods" (Nussbaum 1996: 28). Most importantly, we might suggest that compassion provides a cross-cultural lever for mutual understanding as well: it provides a basis for discovering agreement among individuals who otherwise possess very different value systems. Perhaps people can be morally affected by the suffering of another human being even when they are engaged in an ideology of hatred toward the social groups to which that person belongs.

A second lever for change in cultural values is the moral experience of *fairness and cooperation* as a crucial element of social life. No one wants to be treated unfairly; everyone wants a level of reciprocity from others. Further, social relations work best when there is a reasonably high level of confidence in the fairness of the institutions and behavior that prevails. Is slavery morally unacceptable? We might hope that a culture comes to see the misery and pain of the enslaved, and the fundamental unfairness of the master–slave relationship.

---

[12] Terry Eagleton (2010) also makes extensive use of literature to develop his analysis of the concept of evil.

"If our positions were reversed, I would fundamentally reject being enslaved; this gives me a reason to reject this system even when it advantages me." This is the perspective of reciprocity. Barrington Moore (1978) makes a historical argument for the view that the perceived fairness of an institution influences the likelihood of conflict over its terms. It is entirely plausible to consider whether social arrangements that are viewed as "fair" by participants are likely to generate a basic level of moral agreement, while "unfair" arrangements are likely to generate conflict.

This finding about the historicity of human culture and morality is highly relevant for our consideration of the atrocities of the twentieth century. It suggests the possibility that a deepening of our culture's understanding of the wrongs that occurred, the human suffering that was created, and the steps of social and political change that led to these outcomes, can lead as well to a meaningful change in our moral culture and behavior. By recognizing more fully the horror of the shooting pits of Berdichev and the starving villages of Ukraine, perhaps our political morality will change for the better, and we will have a heightened practical and moral resistance to the politicians and movements that led to murderous totalitarian dictatorships.

This makes it credible that our systems of values and norms can develop through serious confrontation with horrible actions in the past. Therefore historical research, discovery, and interpretation are crucial and essential for the definition of our humanity. We are able to denounce the evils of slavery and massacre today because we have reflected upon the histories of both and have come to see their particular evils.

There is another issue that must be addressed if we are to take the historicist view of culture and morality seriously. What is to prevent the emergence of profoundly repugnant moral and cultural frameworks through the kinds of historical processes mentioned Section 3? How can humanity protect itself against the emergence of cultural and moral frameworks like racism, Nazism, totalitarianism, or fundamentalist religious systems? The answer seems evident, given the emergence throughout history of vicious and hate-based ideologies: there is nothing in the nature of the world that prevents these terrible developments, except the free choices and resilience of men and women in particular times and places who continue to value human well-being, equality, and freedom. We do not need to be absolutist in our moral metatheories in order to remain committed to values like equality, freedom, and human flourishing. Especially in these early decades of the twenty-first century, it is critically important to advocate for and defend those values against the resurgent nationalisms, racisms, and totalitarianisms that we see around us.

The Two Moral Perspectives

Taking a historicized view of human moral cultures has an important implication: since moral systems are assumed to change over time and place, it
follows that different periods of human civilization will have different ways
of viewing and evaluating common human situations. One culture accepts
human sacrifice to the gods, while a later culture rejects and abhors the
practice. One culture accepts enslavement of defeated enemies, while
a later culture condemns the practice. Are we driven, then, to some form of
irreconcilable moral relativism?

When we are confronted with these profound moral differences in our
own epoch, we have the possibility of seeking common ground and providing arguments, based on premises accepted by the other group, that would
lead to a degree of convergence of moral judgment. Perhaps some of the
postwar discussions and debates in Germany about German responsibility
for Nazi crimes fall in this category, and it is possible that some of those
involved came to see the wrongness of their actions. This process would
itself be an illustration of historicist change, and it corresponds loosely to
Rawls's pragmatic approach to discourse over "conceptions of the good"
(Rawls 1993). This provides some possibility of moral convergence and
consensus. Such a conversation is, of course, not possible with Socrates
concerning the massacre of the Melians or Pope Innocent III concerning the
crusade against the Cathars. Moreover, the degree to which consensus is
possible is questionable. However, the goal of establishing a universal and
absolute tribunal through which we might judge the actions of the Athenians
or the French is pointless in any case. Even if agreement about moral
principles and commitments is impossible, it is still appropriate and morally
rational to conclude that Cleon (the Athenian general) and Innocent (the
sanguinary pope) were morally wrong in their actions, given our own
convictions concerning the moral importance of human life and human
suffering.

So it is entirely reasonable to affirm the appropriateness of judging the past by
our current moral understandings. Our current moral and value commitments
are the best we have been able to create to date, and they are the only basis on
which we can judge the practices of others. It is true that the values of the Greeks
of the fourth century BCE were similarly "best" for them. However, we have
a basis for offering a critique of their values, based on our broader understanding of the value of a human being's life. It is perfectly legitimate for us to judge
that the Melian massacre by Athens against Melos was a moral atrocity, even
though the generals and philosophers of the time found it perfectly acceptable

(Thucydides 1998). Their moral frameworks were defective and corrigible. These judgments are couched in terms of the commitments of our own civilizational standards, but we are indeed committed to those standards. This position has an important implication: it is likely that some current practices today, regarded by leaders and citizens alike as morally permissible, will be viewed as immoral atrocities in the future. And those later versions of our selves will often be right.

Creating Institutions

The great evils of the twentieth century were committed by individuals, but the evils they committed could not have been carried out without the workings of the large social systems that motivated them, organized them, and mobilized them. Armies, states, intelligence services, corporations, government agencies – all of these were part of the social and causal processes involved in the Holocaust, the Holodomor, the Gulag, the Armenian genocide, and the rape of Nanking. Moreover, these vast collective evils *could not have occurred* in the absence of supporting institutions and organizations. A Hitler or a Stalin ranting on a soapbox may be able to inspire a crowd of listeners to commit mayhem and pogroms through artful charisma, and violence may spread beyond the earshot of the original spark. But these kinds of collective violence are inherently episodic and limited – unlike the systematic, sustained, and determined murder of eastern European Jews by the Nazi state, or the despoliation and starvation of Ukrainian peasants by the Soviet state in 1932. It is all but axiomatic that large-scale and sustained evil requires a strong institutional infrastructure and organization.

This point invites us to ask about the institutional settings within which such evils are likely or unlikely to occur. What organizational or political resources were available that served to make individuals more prone to act in evil ways against other persons? How does propaganda – state originated or privately organized – work to cultivate the social psychologies of individuals in such a way as to lead them to hate, despise, and fear other individuals? How are anti-Semitism, anti-Muslim bigotry, and racism transmitted into the consciousness and motivations of individuals in a society? How, for example, did radio broadcasts make the genocide in Rwanda possible (Power 2002; Mann 2005)? It is through these mechanisms that political leaders can cultivate a willingness to accept atrocities and engage in atrocities in their populations.

It is evident that the most massive evils of the twentieth century were not self-organized riots, pogroms, or uprisings. Rather, they were the result of determined and documented state actions, carried out by intricate bureaucracies of

murder and enslavement.[13] How were the policy decisions of the Wannsee
Conference of 1942 carried out? How was the plan of mass murder transformed
into *Aktions*, camps, alliances with collaborators, new mass killing techniques,
railroad schedules, and deceptions? It is evident that totalitarian states were well
prepared to orchestrate evil on a mass scale. How did the bureaucracy of murder
and enslavement work in the Nazi or Soviet states? Understanding the evils of
the twentieth century requires us to study the role that state organizations such
as the NKVD played within the Soviet Union in carrying out the Terror of the
1930s, the starvation campaign of the 1930s, the massacres of tens of thousands
of prisoners in prisons in western Ukraine in 1941 (Kiebuzinski and Motyl
2017), and the deployment of the labor camps of the Gulag.

Since our goal here is to find ways of making atrocity, genocide, and evil less
likely in the future, we must also consider whether there are political institutions
that can make evil less likely. What are some of the political and legal arrangements that make mass murder and atrocity more difficult to carry out by
a determined dictator? Timothy Snyder (2015) emphasizes that the Final
Solution depended on "smashed states" and the destruction of the rule of law.
He points to the intriguing case of Nazi-occupied Denmark, where only a tiny
percentage of Danish Jews were killed. Snyder attributes this fact to the
persistence of Danish political, civil, and police institutions (Snyder 2015:
216–217). Perhaps these points provide a clue for the future of humanity: that
it is of the greatest importance to establish and defend political institutions
securing the rule of law.

These questions about social and political institutions and their role within
the "infrastructure of evil" are crucial if we are to envision a future in which
evils like the Holodomor, the Gulag, or the Holocaust will not recur. The crucial
point is the role of a secure and enforceable rule of law, embodying the rights of
all individuals. So we might say: to ensure that great evil does not recur in our
futures, we need to strive persistently to maintain the institutions of law and
constitution that constrain even the most ambitious would-be tyrants. This too is
an instance of human "self-creation": the human capacity to design institutions
and organizations to serve their goals and values.

4 Evil in the Twentieth Century: The Final Solution

It sometimes seems that some questions in history are resolved, finished, and
understood. And then a new generation of historians comes along and questions

---

[13] This is one of the organizing premises of the first major history of the Final Solution, Raul
Hilberg's *Destruction of the European Jews* (1961), who pays meticulous attention to the
bureaucratic organization of the Nazi state's campaign against the Jews of Europe.

the assumptions and certainties of their predecessors and offers new theories and interpretations of these apparently familiar historical happenings. The narrative changes, and we understand the historical happenings differently. Sometimes it is a matter of new evidence, sometimes it is a reframing of old assumptions about the time and place of the happening, and sometimes it is a shift from agency to structure (or the reverse). And sometimes it is the result of new thinking about the concepts and methods of history itself – how historians should proceed in researching and explaining complex events in the past.

The occurrence, causes, and specifics of the Holocaust seem to fall in this category of important historical realignment in the past thirty years. Very little was written about the Holocaust by academic historians in the fifteen years following the end of World War II. The contributors to *The World Reacts to the Holocaust* (Wyman 1996) document the silence that followed the end of World War II concerning the murder of Europe's Jews in many countries and the reasons for that silence. The contributors identify multiple sources of reluctance that interfered with honest recognition of the facts of collaboration and willing participation in the Final Solution – particularly in France, Poland, Lithuania, Romania, the Soviet Union, and Great Britain.[14]

By the early 1960s the central facts of Nazi war against Europe's Jews were thought to be known and understood – horrible as those facts are – but beyond any serious doubt about causes, extent, and consequences. Raul Hilberg's *The Destruction of the European Jews* (1961) was the first major historical study of the Holocaust in English, and Lucy Dawidowicz's *The War Against the Jews, 1933 – 1945* (1986) falls in that early wave of scholarship as well. The two books set the poles of debates that would arise in later years between "functionalist" and "intentionalist" explanations of the Final Solution (Marrus 1987; Mason 2015). Was the Final Solution the result of the intentions and commands of the *Führer* Hitler (intentionalist), or was it the result of the workings of mid-level organizations and leaders who improvised tactics as the war in the east continued (functionalist)?

Recent historians have offered new evidence and new questions concerning the Nazi war of extermination against Europe's Jews, and important new

---

[14] The Shoah unfolded differently in many countries of eastern Europe, and collaboration and resistance took many forms in different countries in western Europe. For example, for Hungary's Jews, extermination came only after Germany's occupation of Hungary in 1944 (Braham 1981). Likewise, the national willingness to confront the facts of the atrocities of World War II in various countries varied significantly. Lithuania experienced almost total extinction of its Jewish population, with substantial involvement by Lithuanian civilians and auxiliaries, but the post-Communist government sought actively to conceal the facts of this history (Levin 1996; Stasiulis 2020: 227 ff.). Stasiulis notes that since 2016 there has been more open discussion of the true history of the Holocaust in Lithuania.

insights have emerged. This section reviews several important new contributions to historical understanding of genocide, mass murder, and active collaboration by civilians of occupied countries in eastern Europe from 1939 to 1945. The section is primarily historical and selective. The goal is to leave the reader with the recognition that we have not yet fully charted or understood the facts of the Holocaust in Europe, the willing engagement of civilians and local paramilitaries in numerous countries in carrying out German intentions, the role of corporations and ministries in implementation of Nazi extermination goals, and the multiple paths that the Final Solution took in different parts of Europe.

New Elements of Holocaust History

Timothy Snyder provides a striking synthesis of new perspectives and frameworks for understanding the Holocaust in his books *Bloodlands: Europe Between Hitler and Stalin* (2010) and *Black Earth: The Holocaust as History and Warning* (2015). Snyder argues that the Nazi war of extermination against the Jews has been importantly misunderstood by the public – too centered on Germany, when the majority of genocide and murder occurred further east, in the lands that he calls the "bloodlands"; largely focused on extermination camps, whereas most killing of Jews occurred near the cities and villages where they lived, and most commonly by gunfire; insufficiently attentive to the relationship between extermination of people and destruction of the institutions of state in subject countries; and without sufficient attention to Hitler's own worldview, within which the Nazi war of extermination against Europe's Jews was framed. These are not wholly new insights, but Snyder is one of the first historians of the Holocaust to offer a synthesis of new understandings, based on a wider range of evidence, of the course and causes of the Final Solution in eastern Europe. Perhaps most striking, Snyder treats the mass killings of Jews alongside the vast numbers of mass killings by the Soviet state of peasants, Poles, Ukrainians, and other non-Russians in the same region (Snyder 2010).[15]

The most difficult question confronting historians of the Holocaust is that of historical causation: what factors caused the massive genocide that occurred in 1941 and following years? The conventional answers to this question revolve around familiar factors: the aftermath of the World War I, the extensive realities of German anti-Semitism, Hitler's single-minded ideology, and the successful efforts by Germany to build a military and police apparatus that was very

---

[15] Alexander Prusin (2010) conceptualizes the topic of mass murder in the period 1933–1945 in much the same geographical terms. Prusin too places the role of state institutions and goals at the center of his analysis of the mass killings of these decades.

efficient in waging war and massacring vast civilian populations. Snyder does not believe that these conventional ideas are adequate. They are all relevant factors in the rise of the Nazi regime, but they do not by themselves suffice to explain the ability of the regime to kill millions of innocent people in a matter of months.

In *Black Earth* Snyder (2015) introduces a new line of interpretation of the causes of the Final Solution by emphasizing that mass murder by the Nazi regime depended crucially on destroying the state institutions of other countries that might otherwise have interfered with the mass murder of their Jewish citizens. He refers to this historical circumstance as "state-smashing" and the "double-occupation" by the Soviet Union and the Nazi state that much of this region experienced (Snyder 2015: 84–85). Snyder argues that a fundamental factor that facilitated the Holocaust was the "state-smashing" that occurred through Nazi military aggression and Soviet occupation of many of the countries of central and eastern Europe. Snyder refers to the double occupation that was part of the period of the 1930s and 1940s: occupation by the Soviet Union of the Baltic countries, the Ukraine, half of Poland, and much of the remainder of central Europe; and then the conquest of these same territories by German military and police forces, beginning in 1939 in the rapid conquest of Poland and in 1941 in the rapid military conquest of much of the territory between the Baltic Sea and the Black Sea, extending to the outskirts of Moscow.

This amounts to a powerful and novel thesis: the Holocaust and the annihilation of six million Jews could not have occurred absent the destruction of state institutions in the countries that were occupied by both the USSR and Nazi Germany. It was the destruction of state institutions, systems of law, and rules of citizenship that led to the mortal peril of Jews in Poland, Ukraine, Belarus, Lithuania, Latvia, Estonia, and parts of the Soviet Union itself. Hitler's war on the Jews was the ideological driver of his policies. But his ability to carry out his plans of mass murder depended on the smashing of the states of the countries it attacked, defeated, and occupied. In this destruction the Soviet Union and the NKVD had played an unintended but critical role during the 1930s.

Why were state institutions so important? Not because they consistently came to the support of persecuted minorities. They were important rather because states establish systems of law, rights, and citizenship. Further, states establish institutions, bureaucracies, and judicial systems that preserve those rights of citizenship. States provided a basis for oppressed groups to defend themselves within the institutions and bureaucracies of the state. The experience of the attempt in Germany in the 1930s to remove citizenship rights from its own small Jewish population – less than 1 percent of the population – was illustrative: it took years to carry out. Statelessness was a crucial feature of the deadly vulnerability of the Jews of eastern Europe.

Why did both Germany and the USSR undertake such deliberate efforts to destroy the states of the territories they occupied, and the political elites who had played roles in those states? The Nazi and Soviet states both sought to create absolute political dominion in the territories they controlled. For the Soviet dictatorship this meant killing the political elites in Poland, Lithuania, Belarus, Ukraine, and Estonia. This motivation explains the Soviet atrocity of the massacre by the NKVD of over 20,000 Polish military officers and Polish officials at Katyn Forest and nearby sites in 1940. The NKVD sought to destroy any possible Polish political alternative to Soviet rule in the portion of Poland they had occupied. And it meant destroying the civic and political institutions of these states. Both Nazi and Soviet murder machines were entirely ruthless in killing potential sources of political opposition. Mass killings of civil servants, mayors, governors, judges, and politically engaged citizens occurred, first by the Soviets and the NKVD and then by the Nazi occupiers.

Snyder's work provides a highly important synthesis of what is currently known about the unfolding of the Holocaust. Another important element of recent research on the Holocaust is the emergence of numerous specialized case studies of specific mass killings, pogroms, and other atrocities committed during the Shoah. These include Wendy Lower's (2021) study of the massacre in October 1941 of the Jews of Miropol, Ukraine, based on careful investigation of a single photograph of the event; Jeffrey Burds' (2013) study of the Holocaust in Rovno in northwest Ukraine in November 1941; John-Paul Himka's (2011) account of the Lviv pogrom in July 1941; as well as a growing number of carefully detailed and insightful case studies based on newly available archives. Vasily Grossman's 1944 essay "The Murder of the Jews in Berdichev" represents one of the earliest instances of this kind of study (2002 [1944]). These case studies make use of new forms of evidence and testimony to gain a better understanding of the causes and human experience of the genocide of the Jewish population that occurred in central and eastern Europe.

Intentionality, Bureaucracies, and Collaborators

One of the oldest sources of debate about the Final Solution is disagreement over the relative causal importance of Hitler's intentions versus the workings of the many agencies and bureaus that constituted the Nazi state in triggering and carrying out the Final Solution. Was the Final Solution the result of a specific plan and set of orders originating with Hitler (and if so, at what point in time was this plan finalized); or was the Final Solution the gradual result of decisions and problem-solving actions taken by mid-level officers and administrators in the Nazi state? Raul Hilberg (1961) was taken to be the most extreme instance of the latter view, while Lucy Dawidowicz (1986), first published in 1975, was fully committed to the former view. This disagreement came to be known as the functionalist–intentionalist debate (Mason 2015). Both Hilberg and Dawidowicz were limited in the sources about the historical facts that were available to them, and subsequent research has largely concluded that neither position is fully accurate.

The limitations constraining the research of the first generation of Holocaust historians stemmed from the fact that the archival records available in the 1960s and 1970s were largely German documents collected by the Allied occupation powers at the end of the war and shortly thereafter. (Hilberg served as a researcher for the Nuremberg trials and had great expertise in making use of these records.) Further, Hilberg was methodologically averse to using first-person documents, including survivor testimonies, which he regarded as unreliable. The result was that Hilberg's account of the Final Solution was heavily weighted toward the bureaucratic decision-making processes that were involved. Dawidowicz's narrative highlighted Hitler's unwavering anti-Semitism and murderous goals. In the Introduction to the 1986 edition of *The War Against the Jews* she wrote:

> From the start, the idea to murder the Jews was just an inchoate phantom inhabiting Hitler's mind. But after he came to power and began to carry out the blueprint for Germany that he had drafted in Mein Kampf, that idea began to develop in stages, synchronized with his other notions for the restoration of racial purity in the German people. The documents amply justify my conclusion that Hitler planned to murder the Jews in coordination with his plans to go to war for Lebensraum (living space) and to establish the Thousand Year Reich. (Dawidowicz 1986: Introduction)

A related debate concerns the role of nationalist collaborators in carrying out the Nazi plan of extermination in eastern Europe. Was the genocide against the Jews of Ukraine, Poland, or Lithuania entirely and solely the work of Nazi *Einsatzgruppen* and regular army units, or was there substantial and willing collaboration in most areas of occupation by local militias and nationalist organizations? And when collaboration occurred, was it grudging and opportunistic, or did local forces in many regions of occupation find their own reasons to participate in the rounding up of Jews and the mass killings of Jews? Hilberg rightly recognizes that the Nazi state required local collaborators to carry out its goals of occupation and extermination; whereas Dawidowicz ignores the issue. How important was collaboration with the Nazi program of extermination?

Subsequent researchers have had at least two advantages over the first generation of historians of the Holocaust. Most important is the availability of Soviet-era archives and records that became accessible in large quantities after the collapse of the Soviet Union. These sources provided a great deal of evidence about aspects of the Final Solution in Soviet-held territories (the bulk of the territory of the Final Solution) that was unavailable through German sources. The German archival sources were limited, first, because Nazi officials made strong efforts to destroy documents in the final months of the war (only one copy of the Wannsee memorandum survived the war); and second, because these sources reflected a preponderance of routine bureaucratic decision-making and only occasional indications of high-level authoritative decisions about how to solve "the Jewish problem."

A second major advantage for Holocaust research in the past several decades concerns the availability of local-level data and participant accounts, providing the basis for detailed case studies of events and locales in the Holocaust across eastern Europe. Since the 1990s historians have given much more attention to the experience of participants – victims, perpetrators, resisters, soldiers, and nationalist political activists – and have arrived at a much more nuanced understandings of the layers of complexity that existed in implementation of mass murder, and the range of actors who were involved.

The debate over intentionality has come to a nuanced resolution as a result of a major contribution by Christopher Browning (2004). In *The Origins of the Final Solution* Browning undertakes to provide a detailed and well-documented account of the decision-making that took place within the Nazi state and military in the first two and a half years of World War II, from the conquest of Poland in 1939 to the battle of Stalingrad in 1942. Browning finds that the crucial decision-making leading to the comprehensive Final Solution took place during that period. Further, Browning and his collaborator Jürgen Matthäus find that neither the intentionalist view – Hitler had the plan of mass genocide in mind all along – nor the functionalist view is fully correct. Rather, Hitler's often diffuse ideas and statements about "the Jewish problem" pointed in the direction of a radical solution without yet settling on a plan of mass extermination; and the experiments in death camps, deportations, and ghettoization that were undertaken by agencies and divisions of the state and military demonstrated a degree of opportunism and organizational freedom. Here is Browning's view of Hitler's role during these two decisive years:

> What was Hitler's role in this fateful evolution? As the ultimate embodiment of Nazi ideology as well as the constant inciter and mobilizer of the party faithful, Hitler had certainly legitimized and prodded the ongoing search for

final solutions. His obsession with the Jewish question ensured that the Nazi commitment would not slacken, that the search for a solution one way or another to this self-imposed problem would not fade away into obscurity or be indefinitely postponed. (Browning 2004: conclusion)

Hitler set the direction, according to this view, without clearly stating what the destination was to be. But countless administrators, officers, and bureaucrats contributed to shaping the final policy. Browning concludes: "In the long evolution of Nazi Jewish policy to the Final Solution, Hitler had been of course not only "champion and spokesman" but also the necessary and pivotal decision maker" (Browning 2004: conclusion).

So Browning's view combines elements of both the "functionalist view" (substantial trial-and-error within an imperfectly coordinated set of bureaucracies of government), and the "intentional view" (the dictator guided and ultimately chose the "Final Solution" after it had been developed and tested). As a human social organization, the Nazi state was itself a complex and loosely linked set of organizations, and a heterogeneous collection of actors and motivations interacted through a period of two years to arrive at a solution that satisfied the Führer.

The debate over the role of collaborators in regions occupied by the Nazi state has also come to a scholarly resolution. It is now clear from a wide range of local studies that extensive and willing collaboration with Nazi genocide occurred in most of the regions occupied by the Nazi forces in 1939–1942, including Ukraine, Lithuania, Poland, Belarus, and other regions of eastern Europe and the Baltic states. The activities of Ukrainian, Belorussian, and Lithuanian nationalist organizations that collaborated with the Nazi occupation have been substantially documented using newly available local sources (e.g., Rudling 2012; Himka 2017; Stasiulis 2020). This fact does not diminish German culpability for the Holocaust, but it does raise important questions of historical honesty in the countries in which willing collaboration occurred. The topic of collaboration remains politically sensitive, since nationalist politicians in these regions have made efforts, through memorial commissions, state-appointed historians, and solemn state recognitions of "nationalist independence fighters" such as Stepan Bandera in Ukraine, to rehabilitate the nationalist organizations that played a role in the mistreatment and murder of Jews, the ethnic cleansing of Poles, and other atrocities of collaboration.

Ordinary Perpetrators

The motivations of the ordinary people who participated in the carrying out of mass murder have become another important focus of research in Holocaust scholarship since the 1990s. A number of historians and sociologists have asked fundamental questions about ordinary participants in the atrocities of the Holocaust: Who were the "front-line workers" of the machinery of murder? What were their motives? Were they Nazi ideologues? Were they coerced? Was there some other basis for their compliance (and eagerness) in the horrible work of murder? Thomas Kühne (2017) takes up this theme with respect to the motivations of ordinary German soldiers. The broader question concerns ordinary civilians in Poland, Lithuania, Ukraine, Belarus, and other countries who willingly engaged in murder of their neighbors and collaboration with the occupying Nazi forces.

The fact that "ordinary men" committed terrible acts during the Holocaust demands further understanding. This historical fact suggests that we need the research of social psychologists – perhaps even new kinds of social psychology – to understand how ordinary people could come to commit mass murder against their neighbors and fellow human beings. This is one reason why the works of Christopher Browning in *Ordinary Men* (1992) and Jan Gross in *Neighbors* (2001) are so important: these historians throw the spotlight on the actions of "ordinary" participants in evil. These historical studies demonstrate the hard truth that "ordinary men and women" can be brought to commit atrocities against fellow human beings. Further, they suggest a mechanism of intervention for the prevention of future atrocities – the cultivation of acceptance, compassion, and respect for the dignity of other human beings.[16]

An important source of evidence concerning ordinary behavior during the Holocaust was made possible by the availability of investigative files concerning the actions of a Hamburg police unit that was assigned special duties as "Order Police" in Poland in 1940. These duties amounted to collecting and massacring large numbers of Jewish men, women, and children. Christopher Browning's *Ordinary Men* (1992) made extensive use of investigatory files and testimonies from the 1960s of the men of Reserve Police Battalion 101 and came to shocking conclusions: very ordinary, middle-aged, apolitical men of the police unit picked up the work of murder and extermination with zeal and efficiency. They were not coerced, they were not indoctrinated, and they were not deranged; and yet they turned to the work of mass murder with enthusiasm. A small percentage of the men of the unit declined the shooting assignments;

---

[16] Philosopher Paul Roth (2004) offers an extensive analysis of three celebrated social-psychology experiments on compliance and abuse (Asch, Milgram, and Zimbardo), and their relevance to the behavior of non-coerced perpetrators involved in mass murder. Both Browning (1992) and Goldhagen (1996) give weight to these experiments. Since the Zimbardo experiments were performed in 1971 a significant number of important methodological criticisms have emerged in the social psychology literature, summarized by Haslam, Reicher, and Van Bavel (2019), casting doubt on popular interpretations of the results.

but the great majority did not. "At Józefów a mere dozen men out of nearly 500 had responded instinctively to Major Trapp's offer to step forward and excuse themselves from the impending mass murder. Why was the number of men who from the beginning declared themselves unwilling to shoot so small?" (Browning 1992: 74).

Daniel Goldhagen's *Hitler's Willing Executioners: Ordinary Germans and the Holocaust* (1996) used mostly the same materials but came to even more challenging conclusions – that a deep and historically unique kind of anti-Semitism in Germany underlay the entire structure of mass murder during the Nazi period. Goldhagen's book provoked intense controversy within the field of Holocaust studies over its thesis of the inherent "Germanness" of the anti-Semitism that drove the Holocaust (Goldhagen, Browning, Wieseltier 1996). A serious challenge to Goldhagen's reasoning is the fact of the extensive participation of willing auxiliary militias and police units in the extermination regimes carried out in the countries conquered by the Germans (Lithuania, Ukraine, Poland, and other countries). This history of widespread collaboration makes it clear that a willingness to murder innocent Jewish women, men, and children was not a unique feature of the German people.

Another eye-opening contribution to research on ordinary people committing mass murder is Jan Gross's *Neighbors: The Destruction of the Jewish Community in Jedwabne, Poland* (2001). Gross provides a case study of a single massacre of Jews in the small Polish town of Jedwabne during the Nazi occupation, but not ordered or directed by the German occupation. Instead, this horrific massacre was a local, indigenous action by Gentile residents in the town who gathered up their Jewish neighbors, forced them into a barn, and burned the barn, killing about 1,600 Jewish men, women, and children. What were their motives? Gross refers to a culture of anti-Semitism at the local level, but he also refers to the involvement of violent thugs from the countryside as well as an eagerness on the part of non-Jewish townspeople to expropriate the property of the Jewish victims. Gross's account provoked intense debate in Poland and was challenged factually, but in 2000 Anna Bikont provided a fresh review of the events of Jedwabne in *The Crime and the Silence: Confronting the Massacre of Jews in Wartime Jedwabne* (2015). Her book is a remarkable work of investigative journalism, involving careful review of existing archives and interviews with a surprising number of persons who were present in Jedwabne on that terrible day. In almost every important detail Bikont confirms Gross's key factual claims.

Bikont provides substantial documentation of the high level of anti-Semitism in eastern Poland (and the Łomża region in particular), promulgated by the extremist National Party and the Catholic Church. She shows that the publication *Catholic Cause* was a frequent source of anti-Semitic exhortations. These conclusions are based on her interviews, publications of the Church and the party, and investigative reports by the Interior Ministry. "In an Interior Ministry report of February 3, 1939, we read, 'Anti-Semitism is spreading uncontrollably'. In a climate where windows being smashed in Jewish homes, stalls being overturned, and Jews being beaten were daily occurrences, one case from Jedwabne that came to trial in 1939 concerned an accusation made against a Jewish woman" (51).

Another important resource on the active involvement of Poles in the murder of Poland's Jews is Jan Grabowski's research on the collaboration of the Polish police in Nazi *aktions* against the Jews (Grabowski 2016). Grabowski documents the substantial role that the "Blue Police" (Polish nationals in a reconstituted police force under Nazi command) played in implementation of Nazi Jewish regulations, including confinement in ghettos in Poland's major cities. This role included carrying out mass executions of Jews (Grabowski 2016: 11).

Significantly for the arguments of this Element, Grabowski and fellow historian Barbara Engelking were sued under Poland's recent libel and defamation laws, created by the nationalist Law and Justice Party government, for publication of their edited book *Night without End* (Grabowski and Engelking 2022) on the basis of statements about specific Polish individuals who were responsible for crimes against Jews. Engelking and Grabowski were initially found responsible for libel against a descendent of Edward Malinowski and ordered to apologize publicly. This verdict was profoundly chilling to historians conducting historical research on the Holocaust in Poland. An appellate court took note of the negative effect that the lower court ruling had on academic freedom and reversed that finding in August 2021. The legal hazards for Holocaust research in Poland continue.

Corporations and the Nazi Regime

There is another dimension of the evil of genocide that has become important in recent historical scholarship on the atrocities of the twentieth century: the role of large business corporations in implementing and benefiting from Nazi genocide (Hayes 1987). It is therefore important to ask the question of the commission of evil actions by organizations as well as by individuals. Moreover, the remedies we might consider are not likely to be the same. It might have been effective in attempting to quell murderous pogroms in Lviv or Jedwabne to attempt to trigger the impulses of compassion, pity, and fellow feeling among the ordinary people who carried out the murders of their Jewish neighbors; but this strategy is patently impossible with regard to organizations like I. G. Farben, Siemens, or

Opel. Corporations do not feel sympathy, pity, or fellow feeling. Rather, they carry out the tasks that have been set for them without apparent moral appraisal. Corporations are not persons; there is no essential "humanity" in a corporation or other large organization.

What were the crimes of corporations during the Nazi period? Corporate actions that went well beyond ordinary business practices included official anti-Semitism, "Aryanization," and the use of forced labor of civilians and prisoners of war. The most egregious practice during the Nazi period was the willing use of forced and slave labor. Labor shortages were a critical problem throughout wartime Germany. Extensive documentation of corporate use of forced and slave labor in Germany and occupied countries between 1933 and 1945 is provided by Ulrich Herbert (1997) and Reinhold Billstein (2000). Workers at industrial companies were drafted into the armed forces in large numbers, and plant managers were unable to persuade the labor control authorities to exempt skilled workers from further conscription cohorts. A possible solution was seen in enemy prisoners of war. The first Opel Russelsheim prison camp was built in July 1940 and was soon occupied by 600 French and Belgian prisoners (Billstein 2000: 47). In October 1941 the Nazi state authorized the use of Soviet POWs as industrial workers under severe conditions of oversight and confinement, but few of the several million POWs taken during the invasion of the USSR survived to be deployed as industrial slave workers (Billstein 2000: 54). In February 1942 the SS central agency approved the *Ostarbeiterlasse* permitting the conscription of Soviet civilians (and later other civilians from eastern European conquest zones), and Opel Russelsheim was the first location to receive a consignment of forced workers from the East. A report from September 1942 lists 2449 forced laborers, including Russian civilians, French POWs, and other foreign civilians (Billstein 2000: 56).

There was also extensive use of forced labor at Ford Werke Cologne. In 2001 the Ford Motor Company completed an extensive review of its corporate archives as well as those of Ford Werke and German and US government sources in a report supervised and validated by historian Simon Reich (Reich and Dowler 2001). The Ford Archive Report provides an extensive set of facts about the use of forced and slave labor at Ford Werke Cologne. Forced and foreign workers made up a sizable percentage of the total workforce at Ford Werke. The Archive Report indicates that "the highest number of foreign and forced workers at any point during the war was approximately 2,000. This peak occurred in August 1944" (Reich and Dowler 2001: 51), roughly 40 percent of the workforce. The report assesses pay rates and living conditions for workers of different national origins, and notes that conditions and pay were substantially worse for eastern workers than western workers. Food rations for Russian and eastern European workers were especially poor. The report also provides clear documentation that Ford Werke made use of slave labor from the Buchenwald concentration camp (Reich and Dowler 2001: 68–69).

How should we attempt to understand these immoral actions by industrial companies during a time of war? There is an emerging field of research in organizational studies dedicated to the examination of "organizational evil" (Jurkiewicz 2012) that is relevant here. In their essay in this volume Jurkiewicz and Grossman (2012) offer a theory of the influence that organizations wield on the motivations, emotions, and behavior of their employees. This account is pertinent to the "normalization" of killing documented by Christopher Browning (1992): the validation by the organization and its leaders of the atrocious actions of killing the innocent offers participants part of the motivation needed to carry out their horrific tasks. Jurkiewicz and Grossman put the point in these terms: "As employees identify with the organization, a stable social system develops that perpetuates the culture while, at the same time, being defined by it. The stronger the culture, the more deeply employees share the value system, the greater the employee commitment, and the more willing employees are to submit to behavioral controls imposed by the organization" (Jurkiewicz and Grossman 2012: 8). They summarize their line of thought in these terms: "Organizational culture exerts powerful influence over individual behavior, because of both the reward structure and humans' need to belong, but also significantly because the individual looks to those around him or her to determine what is right and what is wrong" (Jurkiewicz and Grossman 2012: 12).

In *Industry and Ideology* Peter Hayes (1987) notes that I. G. Farben was responsible for extensive transgressions during the war. It made extensive use of forced and slave labor (perhaps 50 percent of its workforce at its peak); it utilized some 30,000 inmates of Auschwitz as slave laborers who ultimately died in mines and factory near the concentration camp; and one of its subsidiaries was the industrial source of Zyklon B, the extermination gas used to kill more than a million concentration camp victims (Hayes 1987: xxi–xxii). These all appear to be examples of evil actions by I .G. Farben.

Why did German corporations engage in these evil actions? Were corporate leaders of industrial enterprises in Germany themselves fervent Nazis, committed to Hitler's ideology? Hayes argues that business rationality rather than Nazi ideology led to most of these transgressions, an interpretation that aligns with the theory offered by Jurkiewicz and Grossman previously. He writes, "Very few studies still posit enthusiasm for or even general acceptance of Nazi economic policy among the nation's industrial and banking elite during the late 1930s" (Hayes 1987: x). Rather than ideology, Hayes emphasizes "business rationality" as the motivating factor for business executives during the period. Further, he cautions that these same motivations may recur in many other contexts. "The amoral pragmatism and professionalism that propelled Farben's executives dwell within all large-scale organizations, whether they be corporate or political, whether they seek to maximize power or profits, whether they claim to serve the individual, a class, or a race" (Hayes 1987: xxvi).

Since 1998 there have been numerous investigations of corporate behavior during the Nazi period, stimulated by class-action lawsuits concerning liability for slave labor. These lawsuits have led several corporations to open their archives to independent historians for careful scrutiny. One of the fruits of this new wave of research on corporate behavior under Nazi dictatorship is a volume edited by Christopher Kobrak and Per Hansen, *European Business, Dictatorship, and Political Risk, 1920–1945* (2004).[17]

Three war crimes trials took place after the end of World War II involving German industrialists who were responsible for making use of forced labor by conquered civilians, use of slave labor from concentration camps, plundering and despoliation, membership in the Nazi party, and other crimes. These were among the "subsequent Nuremberg trials" conducted by US military authorities and included prosecutions of executives from I. G. Farben, Krupp, and Friedrich Flick. Judge Paul Herbert expressed an important moral principle about corporate behavior in the Farben trial in his opinion and dissent from the majority finding concerning the charge of the use of slave labor and the defense of "necessity" by Farben executives. Herbert dissents from the exoneration of some of the corporate officers from the charge of "utilization of slave labor and all incidental toleration of mistreatment of the workers" based on the defense of necessity. He argues that all defendants should have been found guilty (United Nations War Crimes Commission 1949: 62).

Assessment

This section represents a very selective examination of several important areas of historical scholarship over the past several decades on the Holocaust and the National Socialist regime of genocide and repression. What is most significant about this wide-ranging literature are the new perspectives that historians have proposed; new insights into the location and instrumentalities of the mass

---

[17] Another an important exploration of the moral responsibility of German industry and corporations for the crimes of the Nazi period is Jonathan Wiesen's *West German Industry and the Challenge of the Nazi Past, 1945–1955* (2001).

killings of Jews; new focus on the involvement of "ordinary citizens" in genocide and atrocity; new tools for capturing the experience of participants in these horrific events; a valuable focus on the organizations and corporations that were essential to the National Socialist plan of war and extermination; the importance of state institutions or their absence in facilitating genocidal attacks on innocent populations; and a powerful statement of the vast evil of which a totalitarian dictatorship is capable in pursuit of its goals. When readers immerse themselves in a narrative of the extermination of the Jews of Miropol or Lviv, the predations of Polish or Ukrainian auxiliaries, or the cold calculations of I. G. Farben executives, they reach a deeper and more realistic understanding of the human realities of the Final Solution across town, city, and village, in forests and ghettos, and in concentration camps. And, perhaps, they have a more compelling and personal understanding of what it means, as a human being, to join in the declaration, "Never again!."

5 Truth Telling and Mythmaking

The central question in this short Element is how philosophers, historians, and citizens should confront the evils of the twentieth century. It is clear that studying these processes fully and honestly is a key part of the answer, both for scholars and for ordinary citizens. We need to confront the truth about ugly facts in our history. In his 1944 article "The Hell of Treblinka" Vasily Grossman tried to express why it is important to speak honestly about the facts of mass murder and genocide: "It is the writer's duty to tell the terrible truth, and it is a reader's civic duty to learn this truth. To turn away, to close one's eyes and walk past is to insult the memory of those who have perished" (Grossman 2010: 150).

The central premise of this section is simple. Lies about history play into false group identities and lead to pernicious collective behavior. Historical lies can take the form of outright fabrication, misrepresentation, or deliberate silence about salient events. When Serbs accepted the mendacious narratives of nationalist ideologues such as Slobodan Milošević, the results were deadly, including ethnic cleansing and massacres of Muslims and ethnic Albanians. Lies, misrepresentations, and concealment about the involvement of Catholic Poles in the killings of Poland's Jews during the Holocaust continue to reverberate in Polish politics and authoritarian nationalism. Post-Soviet Ukraine still struggles with achieving an honest recognition of the role of Ukrainian nationalist parties and citizens in the carrying out of mass killings of Jews under Nazi occupation and the conduct of murderous ethnic cleansing against Poles in 1943 (Himka and Michlic 2013).

The section considers the arguments offered by recent historians and philosophers that truthful discovery and acknowledgment of horrible events in the past is a necessary step toward a more just future. The section explores the cultural and political motivations that lead to lies and myths in historical representations, and it advocates for the crucial role played by historians who are committed to the discovery of the unpalatable truths.

Mythmaking and Memory

More than most historians, Tony Judt recognized the power of mythmaking and lies in the telling of history. In "The Past is Another Country: Myth and Memory in Postwar Europe" Judt (2000) wrote passionately about the crucial importance of honesty in confronting the evils of the past. He argued that a people or nation at a point in time have a collective responsibility to face the facts of its own history honestly and without mythology. His points can be distilled into a few key ideas. Knowledge of the past matters in the present; a people will behave differently depending on how it understands its past. So being truthful about the past is a key responsibility for all of us. Standing in the way of honest recognition is the fact that dictators are invariably interested in concealing their culpability, while "innocent civilians" are likewise inclined to minimize their own involvement in the crimes of their governments. The result is mythmaking, according to Judt. The history of the twentieth century has shown itself to be especially prone to mythmaking, whether about resistance to Nazi occupation or refusal to collaborate with Soviet-installed regimes in Poland or Czechoslovakia. Judt (2000) argues that a pervasive process of mythmaking and forgetting has been a deep part of the narrative-making in postwar Europe. But, Judt argues, bad myths give rise eventually to bad collective behavior – more conflict, more tyranny, more violence. So the work of honest history is crucial to humanity's ability to achieve a better future.

Consider the topic of "resistance to Nazi oppression." Judt finds that romantic stories of resistance in countries like France and the Netherlands are greatly overstated; in fact, they are largely false. Here are some of the key and comforting myths in western Europe: the Holocaust was entirely the product of the Germans, ordinary Germans were ignorant of the mass killings that were taking place in eastern Europe in 1941, dictators in Germany, Italy, Spain, and the USSR came to power without the support of the people they came to govern, and almost no one in Europe willingly collaborated with Nazi genocide. Warlike murderous tyrants were responsible for the crimes of the World War II. Judt maintains that all these beliefs are wrong.

This is nowhere more apparent than in the ways different European countries dealt with their own responsibility for the extermination of the Jews during the Holocaust. In the epilogue to *Postwar* (2006) Judt demonstrates that almost none of the involved nations – especially the Netherlands, Italy, and France – have lived up to the duty of confronting honestly the behavior of its citizens and officials during the Final Solution. (As we will see shortly, post-Soviet nations such as Poland, Ukraine, and Lithuania have likewise engaged in systematic mythmaking about the war years.) France's reticence in particular on the subject of its willing deportation of 65,000 Jews created a permanent stain on French culture, and it laid the basis for the continuation of denial of French responsibility by the *Front Nationale* up to the present day.

This deliberate forgetting of national and citizen culpability in western Europe is now part of contemporary Polish politics as well, coming to a head in the 2018 Holocaust law and current slander laws. But Poland is not alone. A very similar process of mythmaking and forgetting has been a recurring part of the narrative-making in the post-Communist states of eastern and central Europe.

Silence about the Holocaust after 1945

Each of the great evils of the twentieth century – the Holocaust, the Holodomor, the Gulag – was shrouded in silence and concealment for decades after information became available to the world. Most inexcusable is the silence that greeted the facts of the Final Solution after the end of hostilities in 1945. The evidence of mass killing was everywhere – extermination camps, burial pits in Poland and Ukraine, first-person observations, the writings of contemporary observers like Vasily Grossman, and the Nuremberg trials. And yet there was little public recognition or discussion of the magnitude of the evil committed by the Nazi extermination plan, and their national collaborators, until the 1960s and 1970s.

In 1988 a distinguished group of experts undertook to write a set of country studies on the treatment of the Holocaust across Europe, North America, and Japan. The results are presented in a massive 1996 volume edited by David Wyman, *The World Reacts to the Holocaust* (Wyman 1996).

Most of the countries surveyed in this volume did not confront their own histories honestly. Rather, they constructed more comfortable narratives that minimized the involvement of their own civilians in the Holocaust, and sometimes minimized and "normalized" the mass killings of Jews. In his introduction David Wyman writes that during the 1950s "the most difficult and sensitive questions about the Holocaust had barely been raised. These issues included . . .

questions about the guilt of the German people, complicity and collaboration in the countries under German occupation, the failure of non-Jews to attempt to save their Jewish neighbors, and the very limited rescue efforts on the part of the outside world. Nor were these issues confronted during the 1950s; instead, in that decade the Holocaust all but disappeared from public consciousness in most of the world" (xix).

The Element highlights an important feature of Holocaust history – the fact that much of the killing, and many of the documents, took place in eastern Europe, in countries that came under Soviet control during and after the war. The Soviet government was reluctant to make available to the public records and documents that could provide a reasonably full understanding of the Holocaust in Ukraine, Belarus, Lithuania, Estonia, and Poland. Wyman writes, "Until the later 1980s these [Soviet bloc] countries all followed the Soviet Union's approach to the Holocaust: they universalized it and forced it into a Communist ideological mold. The destruction of the Jews was seen as merely a small part of racist fascism's murder of millions of eastern European civilians" (xxi).

Here are some of the findings provided in country studies of France, Poland, and Lithuania.

France

David Weinberg's article on France (Weinberg 1996) documents the French government's desire to sanitize the history of the Vichy years and the circumstances of the deportation of sixty to seventy thousand Jews from France to Nazi extermination camps. The issue of return of spoliated property – homes, businesses, other forms of pre-war wealth – was highly contentious in France in the postwar years. Further, thousands of Jewish children had been separated from their parents, and the task of reuniting families was both logistically and socially difficult. But most significant was the political interest that postwar French governments had in concealing or distorting the collaboration that had occurred during the German occupation and the Vichy regime (Weinberg 1996: 18). One result was a resurgence of the far right in France (Weinberg 1996: 19). Weinberg also documents a resurgence of anti-Semitism in French society and politics in the 1950s. He describes the highly convoluted development of French political culture during the 1960s and 1970s, in which anti-colonialism converged to some degree with anti-Zionist, or anti-Israel, sentiment among activist youth. An important event in shifting French public awareness of the Holocaust and the Vichy years was the capture and trial in 1983 of Klaus Barbie, the chief of the Gestapo in Lyons and the prime mover in the deportation of French Jews. Barbie was a notorious murderer of captured members of the Resistance (including the historian Marc Bloch). Preparations for the trial created a great deal of debate in France, and Barbie was eventually convicted and sentenced to life imprisonment, dying in prison in 1991. Weinberg closes on a pessimistic note: French leaders as recently as Mitterrand preferred to remain silent about the crimes and collaborations of the Vichy years (Weinberg 1996: 35), and there has not yet been a clear and honest reckoning of the war years.

Poland

Poland's postwar history was determined by the imposition of a Soviet-style Communist regime. Michael Steinlauf's essay (Steinlauf 1996) emphasizes that returning Jews were unwelcome in Poland, in large part because of conflict over spoliated properties. Numerous pogroms took place in the first two years following the end of the war, including the shocking pogrom at Kielce that resulted in the murder of at least forty-two people (Steinlauf 1996: 112). (Steinlauf gives some credence to the possibility that the NKVD may have deliberately provoked the violence at Kielce.) Steinlauf describes 1956 as an important turning point in Polish political history, the "Polish road to social-ism," resulting in an anti-Stalinist regime that was more pragmatic than its predecessors. But this change of regime also permitted a resurgence of anti-Semitic attitudes in society and within political elites. Large-scale emigration from Poland to Israel and other countries took place, reflecting the conviction by the Jewish population that Poland would never be a welcoming home for them. The Communist government – before and after the change of orientation in 1956 – continued to ignore the Nazi extermination of Jews in favor of "Poles and citizens of other nationalities" (Steinlauf 1996: 117). Every part of this story represents denial: denial of the Jewish identities of the victims, erasure of the Nazi extermination goals of the camp, and inflation of the number of victims in order to suggest that comparable numbers of "Poles, Russian prisoners of war, and other non-Jews" were murdered at Auschwitz-Birkenau. "Auschwitz could thereby emerge as the central symbol of Polish martyrdom, but within an inclusive internationalist framework" (Steinlauf 1996: 117). Even the monu-ment at Treblinka, where only Jews were killed and which is specific about the Jewish identities of the victims there, was described by the press in Poland as memorializing "800,000 citizens of European nations" (Steinlauf 1996: 119).

This pattern of Soviet-era obfuscation resulted in a national narrative "whose effect was to marginalize, or 'ghettoize,' its subject" (Steinlauf 1996: 120). Poland's political history between 1956 and 1989 was complex and contentious, and anti-Semitism played a recurring role. In 1968 the country witnessed a student movement, state repression, and a serious official intensification of anti-Semitic actions and policies, in the form of an anti-Zionist campaign, with the consequent forced emigration of large numbers of Polish Jews.

Steinlauf depicts the period in Poland from 1989 to the mid-1990s as one in which the situation improved. During this period Steinlauf finds that there was a greater willingness to speak openly about anti-Semitism in Poland – past and present. Historical memorials were corrected to more accurately reflect the overwhelming majority of Jews killed in Sobibor and Treblinka (Steinlauf 1996: 144). And Steinlauf records the decision by the Polish government in 1990 to correct the inscriptions at Auschwitz, replacing reference to "four million people" murdered at Auschwitz with this passage: "Let this place remain for eternity as a cry of despair and a warning to humanity. About one and a half million men, women, children and infants, mainly Jews from different countries of Europe, were murdered here. The world was silent. Auschwitz-Birkenau, 1940–1945" (Steinlauf 1996: 145).

Steinlauf concludes with these hopeful words in 1996: "Half a century after witnessing the Holocaust, Poles are freely confronting the memory of the experience for the first time. It is far too soon, however, to speculate about the meaning of this confrontation. It will gradually assume a coherent form only in the decades to come" (Steinlauf 1996: 145). The final qualification is prophetic, since in the past decade Poland has seen the resurgence of nationalist politicians and legislators seeking to – once again – silence honest acknowledgment of Polish responsibility for the killing of Jews during the Holocaust.

Lithuania

Dov Levin (1996) emphasizes the deep culpability of Lithuanian civilians in the Final Solution. Even before the German invasion began, murderous pogroms occurred in many communities in Lithuania, often with provocation by the recently organized Lithuanian Activist Front. "Unlike the pogroms in Russia and Ukraine at the turn of the century, which had been organized mainly by the anti-Semitic and archconservative political vigilantes known as the Black Hundreds, in Lithuania, especially in the smaller towns, Jews were actually murdered by former neighbors, classmates, and customers" (Levin 1996: 333). Only days before the German invasion a massacre in Kaunas (Slobodka) of 1200 men, women, and children was undertaken by "armed Lithuanians who called themselves partisans." Two thousand more Jews were murdered in the same place in the next few days (Levin 1996: 333). Stanislovas Stasiulis writes that "the Holocaust in Lithuania was organized and controlled by the German

Security Police and other agencies, but it could not be carried out without the collaboration of the Lithuanian Self-Defense Battalions, the Police Department, the Lithuanian Security Police, and the local civilian administration" (Stasiulis 2020: 268). After the arrival of German forces and *Einsatzgruppe A*, "Lithuanians were soon accepted ... as auxiliaries attached to German units" (Levin 1996: 333). 90 percent of Lithuania's Jews perished by the end of the Holocaust in Lithuania, the majority before December 1941.

Following the retreat of the German forces from Lithuania after the battle of Stalingrad, the Soviet Union reestablished control over Lithuania. It enforced its party line concerning the Holocaust, especially concerning the deaths of Jews, emphasizing "innocent Soviet citizens" rather than Jews as the primary victims. A quantity of documentary evidence was collected by the Jewish State Museum in Vilnius, but the museum was only permitted to operate for four years. Upon closure its valuable materials and documents were stored in a variety of places, including "book depositories of the Lithuanian SSR, where it was inaccessible to scholars and other interested persons" (Levin 1996: 338). Soviet authorities soon became unwilling to pursue complaints about stolen property, collaborators, and other crimes that had occurred during the German occupation (337). Levin observes that conditions for the surviving or returning Jewish community improved in the post-Stalin period, and there was an increase in publication of books and articles about the experience of the Nazi period in the 1960s and 1970s (340). However, diaspora Lithuanian communities began a campaign of obfuscation concerning Lithuanian responsibility for the killings of Jews (342). Within Lithuania the situation was different, according to Levin: "by the end of 1987 and early 1988, articles began to appear in the Lithuanian press ... severely criticizing past sins of both omission and commission in reference to the memory of the Holocaust" (343). After the collapse of Communist rule in Lithuania the Supreme Council of the Lithuanian Republic issued a statement in May 1990 signed by President Landsbergis, according to which the Supreme Council "unreservedly condemn[ed] the genocide committed against the Jewish people during the years of the Hitlerite occupation in Lithuania and state[d] with sorrow that among the henchmen who served the occupying power there were also citizens of Lithuania" (345). Levin notes the subsequent emergence of extreme anti-Semitic nationalists in Lithuania. He also highlights several important themes or myths that have taken hold in Lithuania that have the effect of misleading the current generation about the grim realities of the past: idealization of the past concerning Jewish–Lithuanian relations; symmetry between Jewish and Lithuanian behavior during World War II; tendentious exaggeration or distortion of proportions; reciprocity in punishment of war criminals; and euphoria about the present and utopian optimism for the future (Levin 1996: 347).

Assessment

These are just three of the fascinating country cases included in *The World Reacts to the Holocaust*.[18] Each case is specific to its own history, but there are common themes. Almost every country had a dark story that it undertook to conceal after the end of the war. The anti-Semitism and pro-Nazi sentiments of Irish politicians were noteworthy and consequential for potential refugees. In Britain plentiful news about Nazi extermination activities was available, but government and media chose to express agnostic disbelief; news dispatches by the BBC from death camps at Celle, Buchenwald, and Dachau "mentioned Jews only incidentally if at all" (Wyman 1996: 610). Post-Communist Hungary favored a narrative attributing sole responsibility for the murder of Hungary's Jews to the Nazi occupiers, whereas Randolph Braham notes that the operations against the Jewish population in 1944 were jointly carried out by German and Hungarian state agencies (Wyman 1996: 217). Anti-Semitism in the United States before and during World War II made strong intervention in rescuing Europe's Jewish population all but politically impossible, and US army administration of camps housing Jewish displaced persons in Europe was strongly affected by this anti-Semitism as well (Wyman 1996: 708).

Both in the Soviet bloc and in Western Europe following the end of World War II there was a residual level of anti-Semitism that expressed itself periodically. In all parts of Europe there were political and nationalistic reasons for concealing or obfuscating the past – for the sake of national unity, for the sake of economic progress, for a desire to move on. And yet each case makes it clear that no country can thrive if it is unwilling to honestly examine its past, to reckon with the inexcusable things that its citizens have done in prior decades, and to commit to a process of recognition, acknowledgment, and sorrow for the murders and atrocities committed in its name.

Finally, it is important to recall that each of these narratives ends in the early 1990s. Much has happened in European politics that has given new force to right-wing nationalism, populism, and anti-Semitism that makes the cautious optimism of the volume questionable. In post-Communist Poland and Lithuania nationalist political parties have competed for power with an agenda of rehabilitating the actions of nationalist organizations during World War II. Hungary's right-wing populist ruling party minimizes the role of Hungary's state in the extermination of Hungary's Jewish population in 1944. These examples fall on the side of "myth-building." On the other hand, there are

---

[18] Other case studies include the Netherlands, Czechoslovakia, Hungary, Romania, Bulgaria, the Soviet Union, Latvia, West Germany, East Germany, Austria, Italy, Japan, Great Britain, Ireland, South Africa, the United States, Canada, Cuba, the United Nations, and Israel.

some signs of greater openness to honest scrutiny of the crimes of the past in other countries. In 2003 Romania established the Elie Wiesel International Commission for the Study of the Holocaust in Romania. The final report (International Commission on the Holocaust in Romania: 2004) provides a wide-ranging and honest assessment of the events leading up to the extermination of Romania's Jews, the involvement of the Romanian state, and the distortions and denials of Romanian Holocaust history that have ensued. The concluding attribution of responsibility is direct:

> The Holocaust was the state-sponsored systematic persecution and annihilation of European Jewry by Nazi Germany, its allies, and collaborators between 1933 and 1945. Not only Jews were victimized during this period. Persecution and mass arrests were perpetrated against ethnic groups such as Sinti and Roma, people with disabilities, political opponents, homosexuals, and others. A significant percentage of the Romanian Jewish community was destroyed during World War II. Systematic killing and deportation were perpetrated against the Jews of Bessarabia, Bukovina, and Dorohoi county. Transnistria, the part of occupied Ukraine under Romanian administration, served Romania as a giant killing field for Jews. (2004: 381)

Investigations and reports of this depth and truthfulness would be valuable in many countries, including Poland, Lithuania, and Ukraine.

Lies in the Soviet Sphere

Stalin's Soviet Union had many great crimes to conceal; the Holodomor, the Great Terror and purges of the late 1930s, the Moscow Show Trials, the massacre at Katyn Forest, the use of the NKVD to terrorize the population, the Gulag, and the oppression of the subject states of the postwar settlement. The Soviet government was entirely deliberate in its efforts to conceal, lie, and misinterpret the facts of its history. It was unwilling even to share the truth of Nazi genocide against the Jews, preferring almost always to refer to "Soviet citizens" rather than Jews as the victims of mass killings. Historical truth was not a goal for the Soviet state.

Andrus Pork makes an important contribution to this topic in "History, Lying, and Moral Responsibility" (Pork 1990). Pork's perspective is especially interesting because he was Estonian and intimately familiar with Soviet lies. Pork opens his essay in a very striking way:

> Scholars' moral responsibility for truth, for the objective content of the results of their investigations, is a somewhat neglected problem in Western English-speaking critical philosophy of history. Nor has this problem found much theoretical attention in Soviet philosophy of history. At the same time the process of reassessing and rewriting Soviet history in the light of glasnost

has helped to reveal the magnitude of distortions, lies, and half-truths in Soviet historiography over a number of years. The process of rediscovering what actually happened in the past has made history (at least for the time being) a very fashionable subject in Soviet intellectual life, and has also raised painful moral questions for many older historians who now face tough moral accusations by their colleagues, the general public, and perhaps by their own conscience. (Pork 1990: 321)

Pork's central concern is the topic of lying about the past. Pork distinguishes between "direct lies" (falsification of facts about the past) and "blank pages" (deliberate omission of important details in a historical account), and he suggests that the latter are the more insidious for the field of historical knowledge. He refers, for example, to Soviet historiography about Soviet behavior in the 1930s: "Many other important historical facts that now surface (like the stories about massacres of thousands of people in 1937 and in the following years near Minsk in Byelorussia) were simply absent from history books of that [Stalinist] period" (Pork 1990: 323). Pork offers a detailed and extensive example of Stalinist historiography based on the annexation of Estonia to the USSR in 1940. Stalinist histories that refer to this case use a combination of direct lies and "blank pages" to completely misrepresent and obscure the facts of Soviet coercion of Estonia. For example, Pork writes that "The existence of the secret protocol to the Molotov-Ribbentrop treaty was usually not explicitly denied; rather it was simply not mentioned" (Pork 1990: 325).

There are many ways to twist the truth and leaving out crucial parts of the story is as much of a deception as misrepresenting the facts directly. This is what Pork refers to as "blank page" deception. Whitewashing and photoshopping the crimes of parties, states, and leaders in the past make it impossible for future generations to design better institutions, act more benevolently, and to avoid the impulses of repression and cruelty in the future. Poles, Ukrainians, and Lithuanians need to know that the nationalist leaders of their past were all too often active participants in ethnic cleansing, repression, and mass murder. Americans need to know that their infantry soldiers were capable of committing brutal murder against innocent villagers at My Lai in 1968. And Chinese citizens need to know in detail the brutalities that occurred during the Cultural Revolution.

Trauma

There is a more intangible aspect of telling the truth about a dark or difficult past: the emotional fact that individuals and groups suffered massive trauma during the Holocaust, the Holodomor, and other periods of massive evil. Several questions arise: what steps can be taken in the present to contribute to healing the victims of past traumatic experiences? And how does trauma sometimes work to distort or conceal memory? The hypothesis offered here is that truthful discovery and acknowledgment of the facts of the painful past are necessary steps on the way to healing the trauma of the survivor. This is also part of the rationale for "truth and reconciliation" commissions and the intellectual and moral thrust of current research on transitional justice (Stan and Nedelsky 2013). How does "confronting the truth" intersect with trauma?

The invocation of trauma is central in Dominick LaCapra's work (1994). In the individual case, a traumatic event must be "processed" – the victim, the perpetrators, and the witnesses all have difficulty in conceptualizing or representing the event without a great deal of reflection and thought. In the collective case, something similar is true – a people or a generation must find ways of addressing what occurred, and this is difficult.

LaCapra's approach to the topic of history, memory, and trauma is grounded in some basic ideas from psychoanalysis, including transference, resistance, denial, repression, and working-through (LaCapra 1994: 43). This is an approach that is especially relevant to the question of how to confront the evils of the twentieth century. This perspective is helpful in two different ways in the setting the history of the Holocaust or the Holodomor – first, as a means of making sense of the thoughts and actions of perpetrators and victims; and second, as a way of addressing the historian's own blind spots, aversions, and rationalizations in the telling of the story. The psychoanalytic categories capture very well the situation of "collective memory" and historians' collective efforts to uncover a narrative of a complex and horrific period.

LaCapra offers insights into the lies of memory about traumatic events in the recent past. He refers, for example, to "the desire to normalize history by having the Holocaust fade into the misty vistas of *la longue durée*" (LaCapra 1994: 9), and he links faulty and false memory to trauma directly. But, he notes, "[The traumatic memory] does not disappear; it returns in a transformed, at times disfigured and disguised manner" (LaCapra 1994: 10).

LaCapra is a literary theorist. How did a working psychotherapist think about the trauma of a death camp? Viktor Frankl provides insight into this question. Frankl, born in Austria in 1905, had the terrible misfortune to be swept up into the maelstrom of the Final Solution. He was an impactful psychotherapist, both before and after the war, and he invented the field of logotherapy. His experience in Auschwitz and other Nazi camps had a deep impact on his view of the human being's emotional life. He expressed some of his Auschwitz experience – initially anonymously – in *Man's Search for Meaning* (Frankl 1963).

Frankl's account of life in Auschwitz is detailed and grueling. He describes arrival at Auschwitz, labor, food, starvation, the cold, beatings by the guards, and severe physical suffering. Laconically he reports that of the 1500 prisoners in the train that brought him to Auschwitz, 90 percent were immediately consigned to the gas chambers. And he speaks honestly about the dehumanization created by existence in a death camp.

> On the average, only those prisoners could keep alive who, after years of trekking from camp to camp, had lost all scruples in their fight for existence; they were prepared to use every means, honest and otherwise, even brutal force, theft, and betrayal of their friends, in order to save themselves. We who have come back, by the aid of many lucky chances or miracles – whatever one may choose to call them – we know: the best of us did not return. (Frankl 1963: 19)

Frankl's theories of personal life satisfaction and purpose were deeply affected by his Auschwitz experience. But significantly, he emphasizes the possibility of remaining human persists.

> Does man have no choice of action in the face of such circumstances? We can answer these questions from experience as well as on principle. The experiences of camp life show that man does have a choice of action. There were enough examples, often of a heroic nature, which proved that apathy could be overcome, irritability suppressed. Man can preserve a vestige of spiritual freedom, of independence of mind, even in such terrible conditions of psychic and physical stress. (Frankl 1963: 74)

> The way in which a man accepts his fate and all the suffering it entails, the way in which he takes up his cross, gives him ample opportunity – even under the most difficult circumstances – to add a deeper meaning to his life. It may remain brave, dignified and unselfish. Or in the bitter fight for self-preservation he may forget his human dignity and become no more than an animal. (Frankl 1963: 76)

These ideas about agency and choice play an important role in Frankl's theories about logotherapy and "man's search for meaning." As Frankl puts it in the companion essay, "Logotherapy in a Nutshell," "Logotherapy regards its assignment as that of assisting the patient to find meaning in his life" (Frankl 1963: 108). Frankl plainly believes that his observations in Auschwitz and his own personal experiences confirm that human beings can seek meaning in their lives under even the worst imaginable circumstances. Frankl acknowledges that only a minority of prisoners "kept their full inner liberty" (Frankl 1963: 76); but the possibility exists for all human beings.

6 Philosophy after the Evils of the Twentieth Century

This Element is offered as a contribution to the philosophy of history. Ultimately, it has a broader goal. It is an attempt to provoke the question, how should philosophy change in consideration of the facts of the evils of the twentieth century?

The dizzying persistence and horror of crimes against humanity in the twentieth century imply a radical conclusion: that philosophy must transform itself. We must ask new and more pressing questions, and we must seek to contribute to changes in culture, institutions, politics, education, social life, and individual human experience so that the evils of genocide, totalitarianism, and oppression are unlikely to recur. The sustained, extended evils of the twentieth century – the genocide of the Holocaust, the Holodomor, totalitarian repression, the Gulag, the Armenian genocide, the rape of Nanjing – require a new orientation to the problems of philosophy.

The most profound questions raised by the Holocaust for philosophy are difficult to see clearly. If we are only concerned with the accumulation of mysteries presented by the events themselves – why did Hitler's Germany choose to carry out genocide against Europe's Jews? How did Hitler or Stalin achieve totalitarian power? Why did hundreds of thousands of ordinary Poles, Lithuanians, and Ukrainians participate in the killings of their Jewish neighbors? Why was it thought impossible for the United States to forcefully oppose the Final Solution when several million lives might have been saved in 1941? – we might say that the appropriate ways of pursuing answers are straightforward even if difficult. These questions require forensic social science. Historians and social scientists need to make use of the best available empirical theories of social psychology, organizational behavior, mass hysteria, ethnography, institutional sociology, and the workings of totalitarian states to provide answers. Each of the shocking facts of the Holocaust or the Holodomor can be studied using the social and behavioral sciences. Historians, sociologists, social psychologists, and organizational scientists are well prepared to do so. All of this must be done.

But confronting the Holocaust requires more than answering these causal, behavioral, and institutional questions. It means asking new questions altogether: questions about the nature of human beings; questions about how to capture, express, and remember the tragedy of extermination and genocide; questions about how to move forward in human affairs while recognizing the pure evil of the events that have occurred. Confronting the evil of the Holocaust seems to demand an inner revolution of self-assessment: what do we as human beings fundamentally care about? How should our political institutions react to massive evil when it arises in the world? How can we rethink the basis of human relations within communities of diverse races, ethnicities, and religions so that violent hate and evil, repression and mass killing, will not occur again? How can we design institutions and laws that would be resilient in the face of emerging evil and violence against the innocent?

Here is a strong way of putting the point: The facts of the Holocaust, the Holodomor, or the rape of Nanking (or the mass killings of Muslims in Bosnia and Croatia, the killing fields of Cambodia, the genocide in Rwanda, or Russia's atrocities against innocent civilians in Ukraine in 2022) ought to have produced a *fundamental crisis of identity* for human beings throughout the world – how could people like us have done these terrible, evil things? How must we change ourselves, our children, and our societies in order to prevent such crimes from ever happening again?

Yevgeny Yevtushenko responded to the Holocaust in much this way, through personal transformation. In "Babi Yar," his powerful 1961 poem of remembrance and sorrow at the fate of the tens of thousands of Jews killed in Kiev in 1941, he expressed that personal transformation in these words: *I am / each old man / here shot dead. / I am / every child / here shot dead. / Nothing in me / shall ever forget!* (Yevtushenko 1991). The poet, a non-Jew, embraced the reality of this horrendous human tragedy into himself; the Jews massacred here and everywhere became part of his own identity. This implies that the poet, the man, was transformed. He was no longer simply Yevgeny Yevtushenko, Soviet citizen, a parochial Russian, born in 1933 in Zima, Siberia; he was transformed and changed. After Babi Yar Yevtushenko the poet sees the world differently.

But this transformation did not happen for most people in the world. Most human beings in 1960, or 2020, had not absorbed the tragedy of the six million Jews murdered in the Final Solution, or the four million Ukrainians murdered by deliberate starvation during the Holodomor, in such a way that it changed their fundamental orientation to the world. What does that quiescence tell us about our own identities, morality, or resilience?

Seen properly, the Holocaust challenges philosophy in many of its branches: the theory of human nature, ethics, social and political philosophy, the theory of community, international ethics, as well as the philosophy of history. Moreover, the Holocaust presents impossibly difficult questions once we attempt to grapple with them. Take just one possible line of thought drawn from the field of international ethics. We might offer a strong principle about a state's duty to intervene against other states conducting atrocities: "democratic states should irreversibly commit themselves to offering unflagging resistance, including ultimately armed intervention, in face of sustained violations of a population's recognized human rights." Is this principle viable within a full theory of international ethics in a world of independent nations? Is it a principle that could be sustained in a democracy, given that it imposes risk and hardship for the home population?

Or perhaps the philosophical imperatives created by the facts of the Holocaust are specific to a nation or a people: "we must take all the steps necessary to prevent the emergence of the threat of hate and violence against some of our citizenry, and we must design institutions of state and police that guarantee that actions of systemic hate and violence will not occur."

The emergence of hate-based populism in numerous democracies, including France, Germany, the Netherlands, India, and the United States, makes it clear that the steps necessary to secure this outcome would be politically contentious to a significant portion of the population.

And what about the philosophy of democracy, the heart of Western social and political philosophy? Do the facts of the Holocaust have implications for how we should think about democracy? Can a democracy effectively protect itself against the political potency of hate-based politics? How should contemporary Germany cope with the rising tide of neo-fascist ideology expressed in political parties like the Alternative for Germany (AfD)? The forces of right-wing authoritarianism are hard at work in the electoral processes of western democracies, and right-wing extremists have won elections to important positions (governors, representatives, senators). Can the arrangements of a democracy cultivate stalwart resistance to the emergence of new forms of totalitarianism and repression? How can philosophy support and bolster the vitality of democracy and human equality?

Philosophy and Human Nature

When philosophy matters most, its importance derives from the honest efforts of philosophers over the past millennia to answer fundamental questions about the good of a human life and the nature of a good society. Philosophy is about values and the prospects for a peaceful, free future for all of humanity. Its most basic problems have to do with how we human beings create meaning and values for ourselves, and how we can create structures of social life that permit the unfolding of the freedoms and capabilities of each of us. The evils of the twentieth century demonstrated that there are dark alternatives that can be realized in history on the largest scale imaginable: mass killing, enslavement, dehumanization, degradation, and totalitarian subordination of whole peoples. How can philosophy address these terrible realities?

One of the central points of this Element is the "historicity" of human culture and morality. Human beings are self-creators; we craft our identities and normative relationships to each other and the world through historical experience. It seems apparent, then, that historians who investigate the atrocious periods of human history have a special role to play: to make vivid to readers the human cost and tragedy of these periods; to uncover some of the social dysfunctions that permitted these occasions to arise; and to help readers wrestle with their own values and concerns in such a way that makes them more vigilant and more compassionate when evils like these threaten in the future.

How can philosophy contribute to humanity's ability to prevent those atrocious outcomes in the future?

First, philosophy needs to aim at greater engagement in the concrete realities of human life and history. There is an urgent need for greater concreteness and historical specificity in philosophical discussions in ethics, social and political philosophy, and the philosophy of history. Philosophy can become more genuinely insightful by becoming more concrete and historical. Philosophers are inclined to couch their ideas at a high level of generality. But understanding the evils of the Holocaust requires us to find ways of making even better use of the tangible statements of first-hand experiences of other human beings. Survivors' testimonies and interviews, travelers' reports, and other first-person statements of what happened to individual people must be treated with seriousness, compassion, and a critical eye. Without the reports of participants, survivors, bystanders, and perpetrators, it is virtually impossible to come to a vivid human understanding of the realities of the experience of roundups of Jews in Berdichev or daily life and death in Treblinka. A crucial part of the learning philosophers need to attain from the Holocaust or the Holodomor is to gain the painful understanding of the individual human suffering experienced by each individual, in the tens of millions. This suggests the relevance of phenomenological and descriptive approaches to human life circumstances, informed by real historical understanding of the concrete and lived experience of participants.

Second, philosophy is forced to reconsider common assumptions about human nature, morality, benevolence, and rationality that have often guided philosophical thinking. The simple assumptions of the social contract tradition – whether minimalist in the hands of Hobbes or more nuanced in the hands of Rousseau – do not suffice as a basis for understanding real human history. It is true that sociality, a love of freedom, and a degree of benevolence can be discerned in human affairs; but so can cruelty, hatred, betrayal, and irrationality. It is inescapable that human beings are neither wild animals nor benevolent and rational citizens. Instead, it is important to follow out Herder's ideas about the contingency of culture and values, and to reconstruct more nuanced understandings of human nature in specific historical and social settings. As philosophers consider "human nature," they need to have in mind the concrete murderous realities of Jedwabne or Lviv in 1941 as well as the quiet and ordinary commerce of Paris or London in tranquil times.

This reconsideration of human nature also suggests that philosophy needs to pay a great deal of attention to education and moral development. How does a human infant develop into a moral human being? What kinds of influences and stimulations help to create the kinds of persons that philosophy calls upon us to become? Can the virtues be taught? Is it possible to help human beings to overcome suspicion, mistrust, and hatred of the unknown other? Can the hatreds associated with anti-Semitism, anti-Muslim bigotry, Eurocentrism, and white supremacy be extinguished through ordinary processes of socialization and education? This point is not primarily conceptual or philosophical. Instead, it requires close collaboration with experts in relevant areas of the social sciences, including historians, educators, and sociologists concerned about transitional justice. The exceptional researchers associated with the *Encyclopedia of Transitional Justice* (Stan and Nedelsky 2013) point the way toward this kind of fruitful collaboration and educational design.

Strong engagement with the horrific facts about episodes of evil within the Holocaust can be a powerful catalyst for moral change on the part of the reader. As we saw in Section 4, Jan Gross (2001) provides a horrific account of neighbors torturing and killing neighbors, and he considers possible motivations for these actions. Is it possible that the readers of *Neighbors* might have gained important insights into the dark possibilities of human behavior, and their own possible failures in similar circumstances? Is it further possible that those readers would have new resolve, new awareness, and new moral resistance against collaboration when ugly occasions arise in their own historical circumstances?

Or imagine the business-school MBA student who read Peter Hayes' (1987) analysis of I. G. Farben and was shocked to learn about the routinized crimes committed by Farben and its directors, executives, and managers. Is it possible that this prospective business leader has been awakened from his or her "routine corporate compliance" mental framework and is better prepared to recognize when the corporation he or she eventually serves may be committing crimes of various kinds? Is it possible that reading Hayes or Billstein (2000) might have produced a new moral awareness of the potential for corporate wrongdoing if these authors had been included in the curriculum?

As a final example, imagine that a truthful and realistic historical account of the My Lai massacre in Vietnam by US infantry (described in Section 2) were part of the training of US combat soldiers. Is it possible that the details of this incident would have sensitized young soldiers to the slippery slope from "killing the enemy soldier" to "killing all enemy civilians"? Would a better understanding of the circumstances that led to that atrocious massacre at My Lai in March 1968 have possibly led other US soldiers to refuse to participate? Could that demonstration of moral courage have also led the majority to refrain as well? And how are we to explain the behavior of Warrant Officer Thompson, who took the extraordinary step of landing his helicopter and aiming machine guns at the US soldiers pursuing innocent villagers? Was Thompson a moral outlier, or did many combat soldiers share his values? Can this secure conception of one's own values and commitments be extended more widely among combat soldiers through better training and moral development?

A third area in which philosophers' questions needs to be adjusted is in the domain of social and political philosophy. Philosophers concerned about defining a just society must engage with the realities of the National Socialist state or the Stalinist dictatorship. The simple formulations drawn from the social contract tradition – citizens and sovereign, state power and democracy – require new attention. How can we design political institutions that genuinely embody secure protections for the liberties and lives of all citizens, prevent the seizure of power by dictators, and embody democratic processes of collective decision-making? What protection does a liberal democracy have against an anti-liberal, hate-based authoritarian movement?

Here too, philosophers must interact with social scientists and organizational theorists in order to have a substantially more detailed understanding of how institutions work, and how a group of institutions (e.g., processes of legislation, lobbying, judicial review) interact to bring about unexpected results. The questions of philosophy – why democracy? – cannot be considered in isolation from the human and social realities that constrain or facilitate various kinds of outcomes. For example, Ivan Ermakoff's (2008) analysis of the decision processes of liberal and anti-Nazi legislators in their decisions to abstain from resistance to Hitler's rise suggests both institutional reforms for democratic institutions (better "guard rails") and cautionary lessons for the political actors in future crises.

These points have to do with understanding the past, in the hope of preparing for a better future. But understanding the *present* is also a crucial task for philosophy – both for philosophers and for citizens. Philosophy needs to help citizens in a democracy to diagnose the malevolent tendencies of hatred and authoritarianism as they emerge, rather than after they have come to full fruition. Further, philosophy needs to provide citizens with the habits of mind of engagement and motivation that permit them to resist those tendencies while resistance is still feasible. If the common human impulses of "looking the other way" and remaining passive guide our behavior when authoritarianism and hatred emerge, it will be too late to oppose those tendencies once they have seized states and political movements. Hungary's citizens have been silent too long for the health of their democracy.

In the year 2022 citizens in western democracies have two highly sobering examples before them that need their attention. First is the plain and determined effort by former president Donald Trump to overthrow the results of the 2020 presidential election and to provoke violent disruption of the institutions and laws that surround the election process in order to do so. The investigations undertaken by the House January 6 select committee make it clear that Trump's efforts, and the concerted, organized, and violent efforts of his supporters, amounted to an attempted coup against American democracy. The democracy of the United States was at its greatest risk since the American Civil War. Those threats remain in the present.

The second example from 2022 is even more terrible: the Russian war of aggression against Ukraine in February 2022, and the atrocious war against innocent civilians that has ensued. Russian forces have tortured and mutilated civilians, executed civilians, targeted hospitals and sanctuaries with artillery and bomb attacks, and have sent untold thousands of civilians to "filtration camps" in Ukraine and Russia. The devastation that Ukraine and its citizens face is vast. All these tactics are war crimes over and above the war crime of conducting aggressive war against a neighboring country. It is encouraging that the European and North American military alliance NATO has provided substantial support to Ukraine's ability to defend itself, but will these efforts be sustained? This aggressive war by the Russian Federation underlines the continuing potential of authoritarian regimes to undertake atrocities against the innocent, and the crucial importance of sustained, intelligent, and effective support by democratic countries for countries like Ukraine when confronted with the evils of aggressive war.

There is another fundamental lesson to learn, which concerns the need for public activism and civic engagement in support of democratic institutions. Citizens in democracies need to be much better prepared to defend our institutions and our values, if the forces of hate and extremism are not to prevail. Democracy is not just about voting in elections; it is about engaging in peaceful mobilization and protest in support of democratic values, and against the efforts of the extremist right to dismantle our institutions. This is one of the values of the political philosophy of republicanism that is given too little emphasis by defenders of liberal democracy.

The underlying observation here is plain: philosophy needs to be engaged in the world we face, and to actively contribute to preserving our democratic values. It is crucial for philosophers themselves to recognize that the atrocities of the twentieth century represented a singular moment in human history: a moment when states, parties, leaders, and ordinary citizens engaged in monstrous crimes, and a moment that must be confronted if those crimes are not to recur in the future. Philosophy must find fruitful ways of contributing to that struggle for a just and humane future.

Engaged Philosophy of History

How do these reflections intersect with the writing of history? The most fundamental commitment of historians is to discovering the truth about horrible events – in detail as well as in broad strokes. Historians cannot be content with familiar and comfortable stories of how these events came to pass – even accounts put forward by their most respected predecessors. Instead, they must be ever mindful of the incompleteness of our current knowledge of the mechanisms of the Gulag, the workings of Treblinka, or the killing teams of the *Einsatzgruppen*, and must strive to find additional sources of evidence and extend our understanding of these various events. Timothy Snyder's extension of study of the Holocaust to the "Bloodlands" of eastern Europe changed the terms of discussion of the Holocaust. Further, historians must heed the cautions of Tony Judt and avoid the comfortable myths of the period – "only committed Nazis committed crimes against humanity," "Poles never collaborated in the killings of Jews," "French citizens gave broad support to the Resistance." It is a key task of the critical historian to replace myths with grounded historical knowledge.

Writing history is not the same as engaging in moral education, and it does not consist in composition of morally satisfying "just-so" stories. Rather, truthful and detailed histories of evil and atrocious actions by individuals and states are relevant to moral education in a different but crucial way. Historians have a crucial and influential role to play in culture-change for successive generations. By witnessing in detail how weakening of democratic norms led to seizure of power by a dictator and implementation of long-stated plans to exterminate Europe's Jews, readers of the history of the Nazi state can gain a much more articulate understanding of where they wish to stand in the events of the future. Would mainstream politicians really want to "de-dramatize" assaults on democratic institutions as "minor," when they know that the rise of Hitler and Mussolini rested on precisely such assaults? Would they want to tolerate hateful, violent speeches by politicians and activists as "just wild talk," if they had a better historical understanding of the fact that hateful Hindu fundamentalist rhetoric in India has resulted in violence and massacres of Muslims over a period of fifty years (Brass 2003)?

Historians too must engage with these large, dangerous currents in contemporary politics and society. It is part of their task to discover, document, and disseminate the ways in which apparently minor erosions of institutions of law and constitution have led to authoritarian dictatorships in the past. It is part of their duty to understand how ethnic violence, genocidal movements, and mass degradation and murder have been facilitated by the institutions of states, along with their ideological instruments. And it is part of their task to focus attention on the fact of "ordinary participants" who are led to commit horrific and inexcusable acts.

Finally, historians have a role to play in the further development of human culture and morality. Political philosophers like Hobbes and Locke can try to work out, on a priori grounds, the logic of sovereignty, majority rule, and a system of law. But a purely philosophical argument about legitimacy and sovereignty takes us only so far. We need to have some knowledge of the experiences of past generations through which both "human nature" and political institutions led to vast human catastrophe. For this task, the historian must step forward; the historian must be engaged with discussions of political philosophy in the effort to chart a more humane and democratic future for all of us, by helping the current generation see the ways in which human beings and human institutions have failed in the past.

Vasily Grossman stood face to face with many of the evils of the twentieth century that we have discussed here. How did Grossman think about the human future, in light of these atrocities? Grossman's writings, both reportage and fiction, are infused with a fundamental respect for humanity and compassion. Here are the closing words of Vasily Grossman's own assessment of the great evil of the Final Solution in "The Hell of Treblinka":

> Every man and woman today is duty-bound to his or her conscience, to his or her son and to his or her mother, to their motherland and to humanity as a whole to devote all the powers of their heart and mind to answering these questions: What is it that has given birth to racism? What can be done to prevent Nazism from ever rising again, either on this side or on the far side of the ocean? What can be done to make sure that Hitlerism is never, never in all eternity resurrected? (Grossman 2010: 161)

Grossman's writings express a strong moral voice. Here Grossman tries to express why it is important to speak honestly about the facts of mass murder and genocide. He believes profoundly that the Holocaust, mass extermination, and totalitarianism must be confronted honestly and without fear. And that is the central claim of this short Element as well.

References

Allen, Michael Thad, 2002. *The Business of Genocide: The SS, Slave Labor, and the Concentration Camps*. Chapel Hill, NC: University of North Carolina Press.

Ankersmit, Frank, 1995. *Language and Historical Experience*. Bielefeld: ZiF.

Applebaum, Anne, 2003. *Gulag: A History*. New York: Doubleday.

Applebaum, Anne, 2017. *Red Famine: Stalin's War on Ukraine*. New York: Doubleday.

Arendt, Hannah, 2006 [1963]. *Eichmann in Jerusalem: A Report on the Banality of Evil*. New York: Penguin Books.

Bikont, Anna, 2015. *The Crime and the Silence: Confronting the Massacre of Jews in Wartime Jedwabne*. New York: Farrar Straus and Giroux.

Billstein, Reinhold, 2000. *Working for the Enemy: Ford, General Motors, and Forced Labor in Germany During the Second World War*. New York: Berghahn Books.

Bloxham, Donald, and A. Dirk Moses, eds., 2010. *The Oxford Handbook of Genocide Studies*. Oxford: Oxford University Press.

Boxill, Bernard, 2017. "Kantian Racism and Kantian Teleology." In *The Oxford Handbook of Philosophy and Race*, edited by Naomi Zack, pp. 44–53. New York: Oxford University Press.

Braham, Randolph, 1981. *The Politics of Genocide: The Holocaust in Hungary*. 2 vols. New York: Columbia University Press.

Brass, Paul, 2003. *The Production of Hindu-Muslim Violence in Contemporary India*. Seattle: University of Washington Press.

Browning, Christopher, 1992. *Ordinary Men: Reserve Police Battalion 101 and the Final Solution in Poland*. New York: HarperCollins.

Browning, Christopher, with contributions by Jürgen Matthäus, 2004. *The Origins of the Final Solution: The Evolution of Nazi Jewish Policy, September 1939-March 1942*. Comprehensive history of the Holocaust. Lincoln: University of Nebraska Press.

Burds, Jeffrey, 2013. *Holocaust in Rovno: The Massacre at Sosenki Forest, November 1941*. New York: Palgrave Macmillan.

Card, Claudia, 2010. *Confronting Evils: Terrorism, Torture, Genocide*. Cambridge: Cambridge University Press.

Chang, Iris, 1997. *The Rape of Nanking: The Forgotten Holocaust of World War II*. 1st ed. New York: Basic Books.

Cole, Elizabeth A., 2007. "Transitional Justice and the Reform of History Education." *International Journal of Transitional Justice* 1(1): 115–137.

Conrad, Joseph, 2002. *Heart of Darkness and Other Tales*. Rev. ed. *Oxford World's Classics*. New York: Oxford University Press.

Conquest, Robert, 1986. *The Harvest of Sorrow: Soviet Collectivization and the Terror-famine*. London: Hutchinson.

Dawidowicz, Lucy S., 1986 [1975]. *The War against the Jews, 1933–1945*. 10th anniversary ed. Toronto: Bantam Books.

Eagleton, Terry, 2010. *On Evil*. New Haven: Yale University Press.

Ermakoff, Ivan, 2008. *Ruling Oneself Out: A Theory of Collective Abdications*. Chapel Hill, NC: Duke University Press.

Forster, Michael, 2018. *Herder's Philosophy*. 1st ed., Oxford: Oxford University Press.

Frankl, Viktor, 1963. *Man's Search for Meaning: An Introduction to Logotherapy*. Boston: Beacon Press.

Friedländer, Saul, ed., 1992. *Probing the Limits of Representation: Nazism and the "Final Solution."* Cambridge, MA: Harvard University Press.

Geertz, Clifford, 1971. *The Interpretation of Cultures; Selected Essays*. New York: Basic Books.

Gibbard, Allan, 1990. *Wise Choices, Apt Feelings: A Theory of Normative Judgment*. Cambridge: Harvard University Press.

Goldhagen, Daniel, 1996. *Hitler's Willing Executioners: Ordinary Germans and the Holocaust*, 1st ed., New York: Knopf.

Goldhagen, Daniel, Christopher R. Browning, and Leon Wieseltier, 1996. *The "Willing Executioners"/"Ordinary Men" Debate: Selections from the Symposium, April 8, 1996*. Introduction by Michael Berenbaum. Washington, DC: United States Holocaust Research Institute.

Grabowski, Jan, 2016. "The Polish Police: Collaboration in the Holocaust." Ina Levine Annual Lecture. United States Holocaust Memorial Museum. www .ushmm.org › pdfs › 20170502-Grab.

Grabowski, Jan, and Barbara Engelking, eds., 2022. *Night Without End: The Fate of Jews in German-occupied Poland*. Bloomington, IN: Indiana University Press.

Gross, Jan Tomasz, 2001. *Neighbors: The Destruction of the Jewish Community in Jedwabne, Poland*. Princeton: Princeton University Press.

Grossman, Vasily, 2002 [1944]. "The murder of the Jews in Berdichev." In *The Complete Black Book of Russian Jewry*, edited by Ilya Ehrenburg and Vasily Grossman, pp. 13–24. New Brunswick: Transaction.

Grossman, Vasily. 2010. "The Hell of Treblinka." In *The Road*, edited by Robert Chandler, pp. 116–161. New York: New York Review of Books.

Grossman, Vasily, 2011. "Ukraine without Jews." Translated by Polly Zavadivker. *Jewish Quarterly* 58(1): 12–18.

Halberstam, David. 1972. *The Best and the Brightest*. 1st ed., New York: Random House.

Haslam, S. Alexander, Stephen Reicher, and Jay J. Van Bavel, 2019. "Rethinking the Nature of Cruelty: The Role of Identity Leadership in the Stanford Prison Experiment." *American Psychologist* 74(7): 809–822.

Hayes, Peter, 1987. *Industry and Ideology: IG Farben in the Nazi era*. Cambridge: Cambridge University Press.

Herbert, Ulrich, 1997. *Hitler's Foreign Workers: Enforced Foreign Labor in Germany Under the Third Reich*. Cambridge: Cambridge University Press.

Herder, Johann Gottfried, 1968. *Reflections on the Philosophy of the History of Mankind*. Classic European historians. Chicago: University of Chicago Press.

Hersh, Seymour M., 1970. *My Lai 4; A Report on the Massacre and its Aftermath*. 1st ed. New York: Random House.

Hilberg, Raul, 1961. *The Destruction of the European Jews*. Chicago: Quadrangle Books.

Himka, John-Paul, 2011. "The Lviv Pogrom of 1941: The Germans, Ukrainian Nationalists, and the Carnival Crowd." *Canadian Slavonic Papers/Revue canadienne des slavistes* 53(2–4): 209–243.

Himka, John-Paul, and Joanna B. Michlic, eds., 2013. *Bringing the Dark Past to Light: The Reception of the Holocaust in Postcommunist Europe*. Lincoln: University of Nebraska Press.

Himka, John-Paul, 2017. "Former Ukrainian Policemen in the Ukrainian National Insurgency: Continuing the Holocaust outside German Service." In *New Directions in Holocaust Research and Education*, edited by Wendy Lower and Lauren Faulkner Rossi, Lessons and Legacies XII, pp. 141–163. Evanston, IL: Northwestern University Press.

Hume, David, 1975 [1754–1762]. *The History of England: From the Invasion of Julius Caesar to the Revolution in 1688*. Chicago: University of Chicago Press.

International Commission on the Holocaust in Romania, 2004. *Final Report*, edited by Tuvia Friling, Radu Ioanid and Mihail Ionescu. Bucharest, Romania. www.inshr-ew.ro/ro/files/Raport%20Final/Final_Report.pdf.

Jennifer, E., ed., 2021. "The Catechism Debate." [online PDF]. *New Fascism Syllabus*. Accessed August 1, 2021. http://newfascismsyllabus.com/wp-content/uploads/2021/08/The-Catechism-Debate.pdf.

Jones, Adam, ed., 2012. *New Directions in Genocide Research*. London: Routledge.

Jones, Howard, 2017. *My Lai: Vietnam, 1968, and the Descent into Darkness*. Pivotal Moments in American History. New York: Oxford University Press.

Judt, Tony, 2000. "The Past is Another Country: Myth and Memory in Postwar Europe." In *The Politics of Retribution in Europe*, edited by István Deák, Jan Gross, and Tony Judt, pp. 293–323. Princeton: Princeton University Press.

Judt, Tony, 2006. *Postwar: A History of Europe Since 1945*. New York: Penguin Books.

Jurkiewicz, Carole, ed., 2012. *The Foundations of Organizational Evil*. Armonk: M.E. Sharpe.

Jurkiewicz, Carole, and Dave Grossman, 2012. "Evil at Work." In *The Foundations of Organizational Evil*, edited by Carole Jurkiewicz, pp. 3–15. London: Routledge.

Kampe, Norbert, 1987. "Normalizing the Holocaust? The Recent Historians' Debate in the Federal Republic of Germany." *Holocaust and Genocide Studies* 2(1): 61–80.

Kant, Immanuel, 1959. *Foundations of the Metaphysics of Morals, and What is Enlightenment?* The Library of Liberal Arts, no. 113. New York: Liberal Arts Press.

Keane, Webb. 2016. *Ethical Life: Its Natural and Social Histories*. Princeton: Princeton University Press.

Kekes, John, 2007. *The Roots of Evil*. Ithaca: Cornell University Press.

Kévorkian, Raymond, 2011. *The Armenian Genocide: A Complete History*. London: I. B. Tauris.

Kiebuzinski, Ksenya, and Alexander J. Motyl, eds., 2017. *The Great West Ukrainian Prison Massacre of 1941: A Sourcebook*. Amsterdam: Amsterdam University Press.

Kobrak, Christopher, and Per H. Hansen, eds., 2004. *European Business, Dictatorship, and Political Risk 1920–1945*. New York: Berghahn Books.

Kühne, Thomas, 2017. *The Rise and Fall of Comradeship: Hitler's Soldiers, Male Bonding and Mass Violence in the Twentieth Century*. Cambridge: Cambridge University Press.

Kuukkanen, Jouni-Matti, 2015. *Postnarrativist Philosophy of Historiography*. New York: Palgrave Macmillan.

LaCapra, Dominick, 1994. *Representing the Holocaust: History, Theory, Trauma*. Ithaca: Cornell University Press.

LaCapra, Dominick, 1997. "Revisiting the Historians' Debate: Mourning and Genocide." *History and Memory* 9 (1/2): 80–112.

Levin, Dov, 1996, "Lithuania." In *The World Reacts to the Holocaust*, edited by David S. Wyman, pp. 325–353. Baltimore: Johns Hopkins University Press.

Levinas, Emmanuel, 1969. *Totality and Infinity: An Essay on Exteriority*. Pittsburgh: Duquesne University Press.

Levinas, Emmanuel, 1981. *Otherwise than Being: Or, Beyond Essence*. Hague: M. Nijhoff.

Levinas, Emmanuel, 2003 [1972]. *Humanism of the Other*, translated by Nidra Poller. Urbana, IL: University of Illinois Press.

Lewontin, Richard C., 1992. *Biology as Ideology: The Doctrine of DNA*. 1st U.S. ed. New York: HarperPerennial.

Little, Daniel, 2020. "Philosophy of History." *The Stanford Encyclopedia of Philosophy* (Winter 2020 Edition), Edward N. Zalta (ed.), https://plato .stanford.edu/archives/win2020/entries/history/.

Little, Daniel, 2021a. "The Holocaust 'Comparability' Debate." *Understanding Society* (blog). June 29, 2021. https://understandingsociety.blogspot.com/ 2021/06/the-holocaust-comparability-debate.html.

Little, Daniel, 2021b. "A Socratic Morality of War?" *Understanding Society* (blog). September 19, 2021. https://understandingsociety.blogspot.com/ 2021/09/a-socratic-morality-of-war.html.

Little, Daniel, 2021c. "The Holodomor." *Understanding Society* (blog). December 1, 2021. https://understandingsociety.blogspot.com/2021/12/the-holodomor.html.

Lower, Wendy, 2021. *The Ravine*. Boston : Houghton Mifflin Harcourt.

Mack, Michael, 2003. *German Idealism and the Jew: The Inner Anti-Semitism of Philosophy and German Jewish Responses*. Chicago: University of Chicago Press.

Maier, Charles, 1997. *The Unmasterable Past: History, Holocaust, and German National Identity*. Cambridge, MA: Harvard University Press.

Mann, Michael, 2005. *The Dark Side of Democracy: Explaining Ethnic Cleansing*. New York: Cambridge University Press.

Marrus, Michael, 1987. "The History of the Holocaust: A Survey of Recent Literature." *The Journal of Modern History* 59(1): 114–160.

Mason, Tim, 2015 [1981]. "Intention and Explanation: A Current Controversy about the Interpretation of National Socialism." In *The Nazi Holocaust*, Vol. 1, edited by Marrus Michael Robert, pp. 3–20. Munich: K. G. Saur.

Moore, Barrington, 1978. *Injustice: The Social Bases of Obedience and Revolt*. White Plains: M. E. Sharpe.

Moses, A. Dirk 2005. "Hayden White, Traumatic Nationalism, and the Public Role of History." *History and Theory* 44(3): 311–332.

Murray, Scott and Christopher John Powell, eds., 2017. *Understanding Atrocities: Remembering, Representing, and Teaching Genocide, Arts in Action*. Calgary: University of Calgary Press.

Nagel, Thomas, 1970. *The Possibility of Altruism*. Oxford: Oxford University Press.

Nechepurenko, Ivan, and Andrew E. Kramer, 2021. "Russian Court Orders Prominent Human Rights Group to Shut." *New York Times*, December 28, 2021.

Neiman, Susan, 2002. *Evil in Modern Thought: An Alternative History of Philosophy*. Princeton: Princeton University Press.

Nussbaum, Martha, 1996. "Compassion: The Basic Social Emotion." *Social Philosophy & Policy* 13(1): 27–58.

Nussbaum, Martha, 2001. *Upheavals of Thought: The Intelligence of Emotions*. Cambridge: Cambridge University Press.

Paul, Herman, 2015. *Key Issues in Historical Theory*. London: Routledge.

Peers, W. R., 1970. *Review of the Preliminary Investigations into the My Lai Incident*. Washington DC: Department of the Army. www.loc.gov/item/97042604/

Polonsky, Antony, 2004. "Poles, Jews and the Problem of a Divided Memory." *Ab Imperio* (2): 125–147.

Pork, Andrus, 1990. "History, Lying, and Moral Responsibility." *History and Theory* 29(3): 321–330.

Power, Samantha, 2002. *A Problem from Hell: America and the Age of Genocide*. New York: Basic Books.

Prusin, Alexander Victor, 2010. *The Lands Between: Conflict in the East European Borderlands, 1870 – 1992*. Oxford: Oxford University Press.

Rawls, John, 1971. *A Theory of Justice*. Cambridge, MA: Belknap Press of Harvard University S.

Rawls, John, 1993. *Political Liberalism*. Cambridge: Harvard University Press.

Reich, Simon, and Dowler, Lawrence, 2001. *Research Findings about Ford-Werke Under the Nazi Regime*. Dearborn, MI: Ford Motor.

Roth, Paul, 2004. "Hearts of Darkness: 'Perpetrator History' and Why There is no Why." *History of the Human Sciences* 17(2/3): 211–251.

Rudling, Per Anders, 2012. "The Khatyn Massacre in Belorussia: A Historical Controversy Revisited." *Holocaust and Genocide Studies* 26(1): 29–58.

Sen, Amartya, 1977. "Rational Fools: A Critique of the Behavioral Foundations of Economic Theory." *Philosophy & Public Affairs* 6(4): 317–344.

Sen, Amartya, 1999. *Development as Freedom*. 1st. ed. New York: Knopf.

Shrage, Laurie, 2008. "Will Philosophers Study Their History, or Become History?" *Radical Philosophy Review* 11(2): 125–150.

Sikka, Sonia, 2011. *Herder on Humanity and Cultural Difference: Enlightened Relativism*. Cambridge: Cambridge University Press.

Singer, Marcus, 2010. "The Concept of Evil." *Philosophy (London)* 79(2): 185–214.

Snyder, Timothy, 2010. *Bloodlands: Europe between Hitler and Stalin*. New York: Basic Books.

Snyder, Timothy, 2015. *Black Earth: The Holocaust as History and Warning.* New York: Tim Duggan Books.

Stan, Lavinia, and Nadya Nedelsky, eds., 2013. *Encyclopedia of Transitional Justice.* 3 vols. Cambridge: Cambridge University Press.

Stangneth, Bettina, 2014. *Eichmann before Jerusalem: The Unexamined Life of a Mass Murderer.* New York: Alfred A. Knopf.

Stasiulis, Stanislovas, 2020. "The Holocaust in Lithuania: The Key Characteristics of Its History, and the Key Issues in Historiography and Cultural Memory." *East European Politics and Societies and Cultures* 34(1): 261–279.

Steinlauf, Michael, 1996. "France." In *The World Reacts to the Holocaust,* edited by David S. Wyman, pp. 81–155. Baltimore: Johns Hopkins University Press.

Thucydides, 1998 [431 BCE]. *The Peloponnesian War,* edited by Steven Lattimore. Indianapolis: Hackett.

United Nations War Crimes Commission, 1949. *Law Reports of Trials of War Criminals.* Vol. X. London: The United Nations War Crimes Commission.

Viola, Lynne, 2005. *The War against the Peasantry, 1927–1930: The Tragedy of the Soviet Countryside, Annals of Communism. Tragedy of the Soviet Countryside, 1927–1939.* New Haven, CT: Yale University Press.

Weinberg, David, 1996. "France." In *The World Reacts to the Holocaust,* edited by David S. Wyman, pp. 3–44. Baltimore: Johns Hopkins University Press.

White, Hayden, 1973. *Metahistory: The Historical Imagination in Nineteenth-century Europe.* Baltimore: Johns Hopkins University Press.

White, Hayden, 2005. "The Public Relevance of Historical Studies: A Reply to Dirk Moses." *History and Theory* 44(3): 333–338.

Wiesen, S. Jonathan, 2001. *West German Industry and the Challenge of the Nazi Past, 1945–1955.* Chapel Hill, NC: University of North Carolina Press.

Wyman, David, ed., 1996. *The World Reacts to the Holocaust.* Baltimore: Johns Hopkins University Press.

Yevtushenko, Yevgeny Aleksandrovich, 1991. *The Collected Poems, 1952–1990.* Edited by Albert Todd and translated by James Ragan 1st ed. New York: Henry Holt.

Acknowledgments

I express my appreciation to two anonymous readers of the original manuscript who offered many useful suggestions about the flow of my argument and additional references to consider. Steven Lukes offered helpful suggestions on the topic of historicist conceptions of human nature. Daniel Woolf provided many helpful suggestions on the manuscript, as well as much encouragement. Conversations with George Steinmetz broadened my knowledge of new research on the Holocaust. The Element is much improved as a result of all these suggestions, and I am grateful to all.

To my children, Joshua and Rebecca, and my grandchildren, Dilan, Davin, Shane, and Rose.

Cambridge Elements ☰

Historical Theory and Practice

Daniel Woolf
Queen's University, Ontario

Daniel Woolf is Professor of History at Queen's University, where he served for ten years as Principal and Vice-Chancellor, and has held academic appointments at a number of Canadian universities. He is the author or editor of several books and articles on the history of historical thought and writing, and on early modern British intellectual history, including most recently *A Concise History of History* (CUP 2019). He is a Fellow of the Royal Historical Society, the Royal Society of Canada, and the Society of Antiquaries of London. He is married with 3 adult children.

About the Series

Cambridge Elements in Historical Theory and Practice is a series intended for a wide range of students, scholars, and others whose interests involve engagement with the past. Topics include the theoretical, ethical, and philosophical issues involved in doing history, the interconnections between history and other disciplines and questions of method, and the application of historical knowledge to contemporary global and social issues such as climate change, reconciliation and justice, heritage, and identity politics.

Cambridge Elements ⲉ

Historical Theory and Practice

Elements in the Series

The Theory and Philosophy of History: Global Variations
João Ohara

A History of Political Science
Mark Bevir

The Transformation of History in the Digital Age
Ian Milligan

Historians' Virtues: From Antiquity to the Twenty-First Century
Herman Paul

Confronting Evil in History
Daniel Little

A full series listing is available at: www.cambridge.org/EHTP

Printed in the United States
by Baker & Taylor Publisher Services